STREAMLINED STEAM

BRITAIN'S 1930s LUXURY EXPRESSES

STREAMLINED STEAM

BRITAIN'S 1930s LUXURY EXPRESSES

A.J. MULLAY

David & Charles

Frontispiece: The face of the 1930s railway streamlining. The LNER A4's front-end was nothing if not arresting, even if an American visitor commented on the lack of painted speed lines. This June 1936 works photograph shows the longer drawgear fitted to the first four A4s after the earlier recessed arrangement (shown in a later photograph) had unfortunately caused a fatality at King's Cross.   (*National Railway Museum*)

Thanks to the staffs of the National Railway Museum, National Physical Laboratory, particularly Barbara Sanger, Scottish Record Office, National Library of Scotland, Edinburgh City Libraries, the Mitchell Library, Glasgow, particularly Murdoch Nicolson and Ian Gordon. Thanks are also due to Michael Joyce, R. B. Lacey, R. A. J. Cox, W. S. Sellar and W. E. Boyd, for advice, information, and encouragement.

A DAVID & CHARLES BOOK
Copyright © A. J. Mullay 1994

First published 1994

A catalogue record for this book is available from the British Library.

ISBN 0 7153 0171 3

Book designed by Michael Head
Typeset by Ace Filmsetting Ltd, Frome, Somerset
and printed in Singapore by C. S. Graphics Pte Ltd
for David & Charles
Brunel House   Newton Abbot   Devon

STREAMLINE

The craze runs rife throughout the land,
Remoulding engine, car,
and even fashions (streamlined ties
are very la-di-da) . . .

Anon *Railway Gazette*, 1935
COURTESY OF RAILWAY GAZETTE INTERNATIONAL

CONTENTS

INTRODUCTION

'A thin line of exhaust would appear over Oakleigh Park and we'd hear the chime whistle as she approached the station. Then we'd catch the drumming roar of a three-cylinder engine working hard at high speed, and see two flickering headlights swinging round the distant curve on to the straight south of the station. The roar swelled to a thunder that almost drowned the tattoo she beat on the diamond-crossing by the signal-box, the platform trembled, and the shining A4 was abreast of us, grey-tinged smoke spurting from her chimney, her driver staring intently ahead. There was barely time to take in the pattern of her flashing motion before she was past . . .'

G. Freeman Allen
(COURTESY OF IAN ALLAN LTD)

The subject of this lively description was the Silver Jubilee, Britain's first streamlined express. Introduced in 1935, its average speed over 268 miles had been excelled by few other trains worldwide over the next six years – when all British streamlined services had already been withdrawn for two years, and despite the increased competition from streamlined rail services on both sides of the Atlantic. There is obviously good reason to believe that Silver Jubilee, and its sister expresses, represented the apogee of British railway operations in the age of steam.

Or did they? Were they not perhaps a result of the contemporary mania for streamlining; a crude American public relations fad foisted on the managers of railway systems already busy enough without such gimmickry? The need to question the *raison d'être* of streamlining express trains is underlined by the almost simultaneous introduction to Britain's railways in September 1935 of two high-speed trains timed at 67mph – the LNER's

Silver Jubilee and the Bristolian express of the Great Western Railway. Despite having to run at almost exactly the same average speed, one train was streamlined, the other not. Why the difference? Was streamlining really necessary after all?

In fact it could be argued that, for the world's largest passenger-carrying railways, streamlined train services were as much an economic necessity at the time – the mid-1930s – as an engineering challenge, being required to divert public attention away from the elitist but undoubtedly exciting prospect of travelling between major cities by air. If it takes a gimmick to secure such traffic, then so be it. In 1934 Railway Air Services were offering a London–Glasgow air journey in roughly 5½ hours between those cities; obviously the possibility of implementing a more reliable rail journey in six hours was worth investigating.

However, 'gimmick' is probably not an appropriate word in this context; the records show that the LNER made a handsome profit on its Silver Jubilee service. Sir Nigel Gresley claimed in 1936 that the train's seat reservations alone would cover its first cost (including the first locomotive) within three years, and all published figures show the train making a profit, with net revenue twice as high as the average. Streamlined locomotives such as his A4 class showed, in addition to hauling lightweight trains, an ability to deal with all kinds of heavy traffic including freight, while it is doubtful if conventional locomotives could have coped with non-stop operations across the Anglo-Scottish border in the years 1938–9 and 1954–6 when the schedules combined with high tonnages to make the services a formidable operational challenge.

Interestingly, in our own times, with the fuel crisis of the early 1970s not so far behind us, and our current (and quite proper) preoccupation with the destructive effects of spent fuel on the environment, it is noticeable that

proponents of streamlining rarely emphasised the cost-effectiveness of reducing air resistance. True, occasionally a technical author writing at the time, reassured the reader that the streamlined A4s on the Silver Jubilee service saved 200 tons of coal annually, but the point was scarcely laboured. Indeed, if there was any *economic* justification for streamlining, it would appear to have lain in its potential for generating new traffic through attracting media publicity.

Nowadays, a modern railway network will attempt to offer a uniformly fast passenger service between major cities, with each train considered as a limited capacity express, probably running to a regular-interval timetable. This is obviously an ideal arrangement for today's passengers but was scarcely possible in the 1930s, or indeed at any time before the mid-1960s on pre-Beeching British Railways. Until wayside stations were rationalised (ie closed) and the number of 'stopping' or all-stations trains reduced, or even cut out altogether, it was inevitable that only relatively few expresses could aspire to offer the InterCity level of service we know today. And in doing so, they seriously disrupted slower traffic – the typical British freight train before the late 1960s had no continuous brakes and averaged seven miles per hour! No fewer than 1½ million hand-braked wagons infested Britain's railways in 1936, nearly half of them privately owned.

The LNER insisted on clearing two block sections ahead of its streamlined expresses in areas of semaphore

Somersault signals on the former GNR main line at Harringay herald the blue/silver combination of No 4492 *Dominion of New Zealand* on the down Silver Jubilee in 1938 or 1939, when the extra coach was included in the rake to increase passenger capacity. The LNER ran high-speed services without any cab signalling aids to assist the crew in sighting semaphores at night or in bad visibility, making the high standard of performance on these trains all the more remarkable. (*RAS Marketing*)

The LMS answer to the LNER streamlined trains was the Coronation Scot, connecting London (Euston) and Glasgow (Central) in 6½ hours. Here the doyen of the Princess Coronation class, No 6220 *Coronation*, is seen leaving Glasgow with the southbound train.
(*RAS Marketing*)

signalling (which was most of the East Coast main line at the time), so it is not difficult to measure the impact streamlined trains would have on such a system. It was estimated that it would have cost £30 million at 1936 prices to have equipped British goods wagons with continuous brakes, but there seemed to be disappointingly little debate on the economics of doing so, particularly when such a modernisation programme would have directly benefitted goods customers by raising freight train speeds, as well as allowing an accelerated passenger timetable.

On its first public outing, its press run, the Silver Jubilee caught up with, no farther north than Grantham, an express which had left London 45 minutes before it. Yet the latter was powered by a locomotive almost as powerful and as fast as *Silver Link*. In other words, the advent of the streamlined express was a concrete admission by the railways that they could offer a far better service to their customers, and were attempting to do so only while very much under the threat of losing passengers to the private car or even the aeroplane.

Nor is this conclusion the exclusive product of hindsight. Writing in 1928, the controversial railway author Robert Collier (Baron Monkswell), argued that from about 1850 Britain's railways had quite intentionally ceased to compete with one another, on the cosy presumption that they had no terrestrial transport rivals, except one another. In a book published 15 years earlier, Monkswell had commented on the slow speed of Anglo-Scottish expresses at that time; but by the time of his 1928 publication (see the Bibliography), they were actually *slower*.

1 FROM DA VINCI TO DALBY

When did the concept of streamlining evolve? Some historians trace its beginnings in the works of Leonardo da Vinci and Newton, although the theory of air resistance to a moving object is believed to have been first studied by Leonhard Euler in 1755, and the word 'streamline' itself had been coined by the 1870s, according to the *Oxford English Dictionary*. The emergence of the Class C 4–4–0, with its 'wind-cutter' smokebox, on France's PLM railway in the 1890s was material proof that locomotive designers were aware of the rudiments of air resistance – and how to minimise it – long before streamlining became prevalent, even fashionable, after World War I.

Railway streamlining has an intriguing 'pre-history'. In 1825, the very year when Stephenson's *Locomotion No 1* first trundled from Stockton to Darlington, a Scottish newspaper editor named Charles MacLaren wrote

'the resistance of the air which, in vulgar apprehension, passes for nothing, comes to be the greatest impediment to the motion of the (railway) vehicles, and may in some cases absorb five parts in six of the whole power'.

It was an astonishing statement by one who was hardly writing from his own experience – since few humans had then broken the 30mph speed barrier – but this apologist for railways was inaccurate only to a matter of degree.

The theory of the air resistance of railway stock was first researched in detail by one Dr Dionysius Lardner, FRS, who presented two papers on the subject to the recently instituted British Association for the Advancement of Science in 1838 and again in 1841. His first paper indicates that the matter had previously been studied by Euler and others principally in connection with the science of ballistics, but he believed that air was one of four varieties of resistance to the movement of a railway

vehicle; the others were friction of axles in their bearings, tyres on the rail surface, and flanges intermittently in contact with the rail.

Lardner's second paper is quite extraordinary, describing a series of experiments designed to measure air resistance, and other inhibitors to movement, on an unpowered train rolling freely downhill on a 1 in 89 gradient on the Liverpool & Manchester Railway. Its locomotive, named *Fury*, had its pistons and rods removed for the test, and the speed was measured as the train passed stakes driven into the ground every 110yds. More copious tests were also conducted on the Grand Junction Railway, engine *Hecla* and its train running the 95 miles between Liverpool and Birmingham in 187 minutes net. The resulting log is one detailed enough to satisfy anyone interested in locomotive performance. Lardner appears to have drawn negative conclusions on the need for streamlining – 'expedients for attaching a sharp front to the engine are ineffectual and useless' – not surprisingly considering the low speeds being attained on test and the lack of controlled conditions and recording apparatus.

Nevertheless, railway histories reveal precursors of streamlined railway vehicles to delight the transport antiquarian, none more so than a locomotive designed with a ship's bow at each end around 1837. This was the brainchild of Thomas Cochrane, the tenth Earl of Dundonald who, after a highly courageous war career and a sensational public trial (and acquittal) for corruption, entered his advancing years in the 1830s determined to convert the traditionally-minded Royal Navy to steam power. This was no easy matter and so to keep in practice, as it were, he arranged to have one of his patented boilers mounted on a locomotive on the then still incomplete London & Greenwich Railway. An engineering apprentice of the time, Frederick Bramwell (who was afterwards knighted), recalled later, in a comment which he made to the Institution of Civil Engineers, that

'the old sailor had said he was not going to have his engine stopped by the wind, or to have a flat bow, and he had a sharp boat-bow fitted at each end of his engine'.

Another source suggests that the line's No 3 locomotive *Princess Victoria*, built by Braithwaite & Milner, was to be given a shiplike profile, but his was apparently to fit in with the line's marine associations, and was presumably different from the Cochrane experiment. Unfortunately, it appeared that Cochrane's patented boiler could not be properly seated on the frames, so the world's first streamlined locomotive had to wait the best part of another century before it could make its appearance.

More theoretical work on the resistance of railway vehicles was conducted by William Rankine, Professor of Civil Engineering at Glasgow University. In his 1859 publication *A Manual of the Steam Engine*, Rankine gives a formula for the calculation of all sources of resistance on rail vehicles, arguing that this should apply only at speeds above 10mph, as 'resistance is sensibly constant below that speed'. Rankine did not however appear to suggest any design changes to minimise resistance, and cited as an expert on the matter, interestingly, 'Mr Gooch' for his work 'on the broad gauge'.

The next proposed streamlined train concept to be considered was one patented in the USA by the Reverend Samuel Calthrope in August 1865. US Patent document No 49,227 shows a 4–4–0 or possibly 4–2–2–0 steam locomotive with a wedge-like prow and flared lines almost down to rail level. The frontal effect was spoiled by a typically mid-Victorian vertical chimney but the rear of the articulated coaching stock shows an aerodynamically rounded appearance. This English-born cleric never saw his creation in action but his vision was a prophetic one, not least because he appeared to be advocating the horizontal wedge shape made famous by the Bugatti railcars and the LNER A4. Equally, Sir Henry Bessemer, principally remembered for his innovatory steel foundry techniques, suggested, around 1847, that the space between railway coaches could be eliminated by leather aprons stretched between each vehicle's roof – an idea to find its time some 85 years later.

The period between the World Wars I and II was the Streamlined Age. When applying its precept to railway

design and operation, art and science proved quite inseparable. Hand in hand with the intention of making vehicles faster went the idea of making the vehicle *look* faster, with attendant favourable publicity. And publicity was suddenly something railway managements had to take into account – the invention of radio broadcasting, cinema newsreels, and the proliferation of illustrated magazines meant that the appearance and character of locomotives and trains had to be newsworthy or attractive, or both. (Nor was television all that far in the future when our story opens – the first down Coronation streamliner was televised leaving London.) After all, no

The object of much artistic appraisal, the LNER's W1 4–6–4 was in fact a technical experiment to assess the practicability of using a high-pressure marine boiler in railway conditions. Here the unique No 10000 enters Darlington with an up express in June 1930, complete with dynamometer car.   (*RAS Marketing*)

railway or airline operator would intentionally want its passenger vehicles to look *slow*, and this applied equally to car manufacturers.

It was the last-named who appear to have provided the catalyst for the Streamline Explosion. To challenge

Sir Nigel Gresley on the footplate of his A4 Pacific No 4489 *Dominion of Canada* just before its naming ceremony at King's Cross in June 1937.   (*RAS Marketing*)

the utilitarian but unpretentious Model T Ford for the new mass market for transport that was opening up in the USA in the 1920s – car ownership increased by a staggering factor of 36 over the 20 years before 1930 – the General Motors Corporation took advice on the visual appearance of its products. Not only did this awareness of industrial design cause an escalation in private transport, it gave the railroads in the USA good reason to review the services they were offering. And there sprang up a group of freelance streamliners: Norman Bel Geddes, Raymond Loewy, Otto Kuhler and others. They would be commissioned to advise on the design of anything from a department store window display to a train. The age of the industrial designer was born.

As far as British locomotive engineers were concerned, it seems that they had been streamlining their products for years without realising it! Contemporary American authors commented on the tradition for British steam locomotives to have a distinctive and highly favourable visual appearance. Great Western admirers will know instinctively what this entailed, but almost any British railway before World War I, with its distinctive livery kept clean by dedicated footplate staff, made a positive corporate impression. To American and continental eyes, British steam locomotives looked streamlined before the word was thought of – the lack of auxiliary fittings attached to the exterior of the average engine gave a smooth, uncluttered, appearance. The Great Northern 'Single' was a case in point; the boiler did not even carry a dome!

So when in 1929 Nigel Gresley produced his 'Hush-Hush' 4–6–4 No 10000 for the LNER, he unconsciously prompted at least one American designer to describe the engine as 'semi-streamlined', and it makes an appearance in Bel Geddes's book *Horizons* (with Britain's greatest exponent of streamlined train travel mis-spelt as H. N. Grisley!). Raymond Loewy, French-born designer of streamlined steam and electric locos for the Pennsylvania Railroad, was less complimentary about No 10000's appearance, believing that horizontal lining would have improved it. In the same book on locomotive aesthetics (see the Bibliography), Loewy described the first A4 *Silver Link* as 'somewhat lacking in grace', but surprisingly he enthused about the bulbous protuberances on the smokeboxes on one member each of the Great Western King and Castle classes, something that was less well received by Swindon aficionados.

Indeed, streamlining has such a would-be aesthetic aspect to it, that subjective opinion about it constantly occurs in the literature of the subject. This author hopes that readers will bear with his own expressed opinions about the appearance of particular locomotives; just as many opinions from American sources about the appearance of British streamlined steam range from the intuitive to the eccentric. In particular, American eyes failed to appreciate that British steam engines were 'simplified' in appearance – in lacking unsightly pipework and plumbing on the exterior of the boiler casing – for a very good functional, rather than an aesthetic, reason.

For the truth of the matter was that the British loading gauge was so limited, compared to almost any other in the world, that no large excrescences on the boiler or running boards were possible anyway. In the case of No 10000, Gresley was experimenting with the use of a high pressure marine type boiler which required to be mounted as high above the frames as possible. This necessitated the use of a shortened, indeed almost non-existent, chimney, so Gresley took advice from an academic, believed to be Professor W. E. Dalby, in designing the new locomotive's front end in order to remove exhaust steam from the driver's vision. The almost square appearance of the cab shows that there was no streamlining intention in Gresley's mind in 1929, yet his products were being viewed by design critics as if they were paintings or some kind of kinetic sculpture!

Nevertheless Gresley was to become the greatest proponent of streamlining in Britain, and arguably anywhere in the world. In the five years before the USA entered World War II, the LNER's three streamlined expresses, the Silver Jubilee, the Coronation, and West Riding Limited ranked high in terms of world rail speed over an entire journey (as opposed to point-to-point times), whether propulsion was electric, steam, diesel locomotive or diesel railcar. No other long-distance (150 miles or more) British trains entered this elite, while Gresley's products held their placings even though they were mothballed in August 1939, more than two years before their American rivals were affected by war. Not only that, Gresley's streamlined locomotives were hauling express trains as late as 1966, long after steam, streamlined or not, had vanished from US railroads.

To sum up, the 1930s vogue for streamlining fitted the British railway locomotive like a glove. The same cannot be said for the concept of running streamline trains through densely trafficked systems such as the East and West Coast main lines between London and Scotland, but run they did, and rapidly staked a claim as representing the summit of British railway operations, certainly in the Steam Age.

This is their story.

2 STREAMLINING – THE WORLD VIEW

Art historians may regard the late 1920s and early 1930s as the Streamline Age, but its application to the world of railways was introduced, ironically, at almost a snail's pace. It seems to have begun, as so many fashionable ideas do, in the USA, when in the autumn of 1931 the Philadelphia & Western Railroad introduced an electric railcar (third rail, 600 volts dc) to operate its Philadelphia–Norristown route in the hitherto unprecedented time of 17 minutes for the 14 miles including three stops. The aluminium bodied car, weighing 23 tons tare, was built by the J. G. Brill Company and had its ends designed to minimise wind resistance after 30 different configurations had been tested in a wind tunnel at the University of Michigan. Ten such cars were introduced on the route between Norristown and the 69th Street terminal in Upper Darby as an answer to competition from the rival Pennsylvania Railroad services.

The Brill cars proved to have a long life, working the Philadelphia suburbs for nearly 60 years before becoming due for replacement on what is now the South Eastern Pennsylvania Transportation Authority (SEPTA) by German-supplied cars in late 1989, but they did not hold their streamlined lead for long. Research into overcoming the air resistance of moving vehicles was under way in Germany, and the resulting streamlined railcar is usually acknowledged as the pioneer in the field. Only a few months after the Norristown commuters began experiencing the sensation of streamlined transport in March 1932, a Maybach-powered diesel railcar was outshopped in Germany intended to transport 102 passengers in its articulated two-car 133ft length. It was to be operated on the 178 mile Berlin–Hamburg route at a mile a minute – or so the technical press was told at that time. Powered by two 410bhp motors, the railcar set in fact covered the distance in only 142 minutes just before Christmas, an average of 75mph, and enough for the world to glimpse the potential of this new type of motive power.

The French were determined not to be left behind, the État system ordering two single coach diesel railcars from private manufacturers, their most interesting characteristics being their wedge-like end profiles. This design was by Ettore Bugatti, and showed considerable reliance on his racing car experience. Bugatti was the son of a Milanese furniture designer who was fascinated by mechanical objects, and rapidly forged for himself a reputation for the futuristic design of automobiles. Any railway enthusiasts seeing the design for the wedge-profiled bonnet of his 1923 Type 32 Tank racing car will know which British steam locomotive borrowed the idea twelve years later!

Seventy-six feet long, the 800 horsepower for the Bugatti railcar came from four transversely-aligned automobile engines, and the 52 seater cars had the driver's cab in the middle of the vehicle, the driver commanding a lookout from a 'birdcage' halfway along the roof. Quaint though this looked, 107mph was soon clocked up on trial, and a 500 mile non-stop endurance run accomplished. It was intended to introduce the cars on the Paris–Deauville service (136 miles in two hours), while the PLM railway, which had operated 'wind-cutting' steam locomotives in the previous century, announced plans for its own lightweight railcars.

Meanwhile, the German railcar was being timetabled to operate the *Fliegende Hamburger* service, from Berlin Lehrter to Hamburg Hauptbahnhof, 178 miles, in 138 minutes, and 140 minutes in the opposite direction, at average speeds of 77.4mph and 76.3mph respectively. This timetable was intended to operate from March 1933 although in fact 15 May was the opening day, the cars having been 'temporarily withdrawn' in March, with no reason given. In passing, it is interesting to note that a steam-hauled short train of three vehicles was used as a reserve contingency if a diesel was not available for the 8.02am ex Berlin (11.00am from December 1933) and the 3.16pm return. It was soon found that a Class 0.3

Pacific could regularly achieve, with no streamlining and a greater passenger capacity, a 148 minute journey.

On 21 March 1933, after the *Fliegende Hamburger* had announced itself to the technical press, but before it had entered commercial service, the chief general manager of Britain's LNER, Sir Ralph Wedgwood, dictated a memo for the company's Superintendents' Committee to discuss. In it, he asked them 'to consider the problems involved in timing and finding paths for units of this description . . . say between London and Edinburgh with a stop at Newcastle, or between London and Leeds non-stop'. The speed mooted by Wedgwood was 90mph, presumably a maximum, but he did not specify what kind of motive power would be required.

Speculation was being aired in the technical press as to whether diesel- and petrol-engined railcars could rival aircraft on shorter point-to-point journeys – there seemed to be no public consideration at this stage of steam achieving such speed summits. Indeed, in January 1934 the *Railway Gazette* commented

'The tendency nowadays is to abandon the idea [of streamlining] in so far as locomotives are concerned, at least in its more pronounced form, but to extend its use in the case of self-propelled cars, especially those designed for high-speed work.'

However, the editorial went on to predict that steam could find a place in the exciting new world of high-speed streamlined operations, a fact soon to be borne out in practice – and in a most unexpected part of the world.

Of all places where the first streamlined steam service came into operation, it was not to be in the USA, nor in Europe. It was in fact in Manchukuo or South Manchuria that the concept of the steam-hauled streamlined express train was first set to work. This was an area of what is now China which had been invaded by the Japanese in about 1906 and treated effectively as a mainland Japanese colony, complete with a puppet dictator. The bulk of the oppressed population were virtually peasants, and the land was only beginning to be developed, partly through the spread of Japanese-built railways. These obviously had a military significance as the Japanese hoped to annex more territory from Korea, the Soviet Union (not then a superpower) and China. The 150 mile Hsingking–Harbin line was converted from the Russian 5ft 0in gauge to Standard by the invaders on 31 August 1935 – in three hours! Similarly, a high-speed train service from the coast into the centre of Manchukuo was useful to the colonial administrators, as well as being a symbol of Japanese technical progress.

Otherwise, the sight of a crack streamlined express, replete with air conditioning and an observation parlour, running in such an unhappy country is scarcely credible, and was not made any the less so by the circumstances of its construction. Two streamlined Pacifics were built in Japan for the service and then dismantled, shipped to the Chinese mainland, and reassembled in the Shakako works of the South Manchurian Railway. Details of the locomotives were simply not available in the technical press of the time, (in fact, 78.7in driving wheels, 220 lb/sq in boiler, machine stoker), although more was known about the coaching stock. Six air-conditioned light green coaches were constructed on frames 80.5ft long (24ft longer than the stock of the Silver Jubilee) in aluminium on high-tensile steel frames (the LNER used teak bodies), running on SKF roller bearings (not copied by Doncaster). Connecting the Pacific port of Dairen (Dalian) and Hsingking, 438 miles in 510 minutes, an average overall speed of 51.5mph was achieved, including one stop. Hsingking is now known as Changchun, the provincial capital of Jilin in China. This pioneering streamlined steam service, the Asia Express, began on 1 November 1934.

* * *

The world's second streamlined steam service went into regular fare-earning service in 1935, six months after the Asia Express. The United States provided the second example of such a train; indeed, as streamlining became such an integral feature of American railroad design and operation from about 1933 to 1950, it is appropriate to consider its history separately, if briefly, even at the risk of breaking the chronology of the streamline story.

It is a measure of how much United States railroads were caught up by the streamline craze that more than a hundred services were introduced in the ten years before World War II (which began on 7 December 1941 as far as the USA was concerned). This figure includes all types of motive power and varying degrees of physical streamlining, some of them, it must be said, quite negligible in outline. Of the five streamlined services, three of them steam-powered, inaugurated before the introduction of the Silver Jubilee on to British metals in September 1935, one was the Abraham Lincoln of the Baltimore & Ohio. In fact to non-American eyes the two 4–4–4s operating this Chicago–St Louis service were no more streamlined than a Gresley A3; the train engine had as many domes and feed pipes above the boiler as two or three Great Western Kings put together!

The lengthy list of American streamlined services is a dizzying one. How many British rail enthusiasts have heard of the Egyptian Zipper of the Chicago & Eastern Illinois, the Cracker (Southern), or the Lark (Southern Pacific)? Of these three taken at random, only one was steam-powered; indeed, despite steam's hitherto dominant position on US railroads only 40 per cent of American streamlined services were so powered – and in some cases for only part of the train's history – so it seems obvious that, to many railroad managements, streamlining was synonymous with newer forms of motive power. By 1937 two US firms, General Electric and Electromotive, were offering main line diesel locomotive units with streamlined bodies, often under special hire purchase arrangements. In the circumstances it is perhaps surprising that new streamlined steam services were still being introduced as late as Pearl Harbor Day 1941 (New York Central's Empire State Express), and new individual steam locomotives ordered with streamlined casings as late as 1950 (Norfolk & Western).

Streamlining on American railroads was often a fairly casual engineering adjustment – locomotives already 30 years old suddenly appeared in wind-cheating casings (something similar happened in France). More than one locomotive class was clad thus, at the initiative of the line's own engineers, with no designer being involved (Frisco Lines, Reading Company). One entire train was streamlined purely for lease as an exhibition train (New York Central's Rexall train), while one locomotive sported two entirely different streamlined casings, one after the other, in no more than five years (NYC's Commodore Vanderbilt). The Rutland Railroad, deep in receivership, even at-

tempted to reverse its fortunes by introducing a streamlined freight train, The Whippet.

There is comparatively little evidence of US railway streamlining having any scientific basis; the story of American streamlined steam is one often bereft of wind tunnel experiments after those originally conducted on the Brill railcar, or of comparative fuel consumption trials between similarly powered streamlined and conventional locomotives of similar power, as happened in France. Appearance seemed to be the all-important factor; such locomotive casings as those designed by Raymond Loewy for the Pennsylvania Railroad or Henry Dreyfuss for the New York Central were built almost straight from the designer's imagination; their originators, far from having engineering qualifications, normally specialised in designing shop window displays or theatre backdrops. As a result, basic engineering needs – such as a supply of cool air to reciprocating parts – were sometimes ignored, but nobody could ever describe American streamlined steam as lacking in excitement!

But to return to a chronological account of US streamlining.

One American transport historian credits the New York Central's Commodore Vanderbilt as being the first steam streamlined express locomotive, although it appears to have been just beaten by the Japanese-built engines for Manchuria, and was in any event not hauling a streamlined train. (Its normal working, the prestigious Twentieth Century Limited, was not so treated until 1938.) It was on the tracks of the Milwaukee Road westwards from Chicago, and in direct competition with the new Zephyr diesels, that such a train hit the headlines.

On 29 May 1935 the Hiawatha express of the Chicago, Milwaukee, St Paul & Pacific Railroad began running the 410 miles between Chicago and St Paul in 390 minutes, inclusive of five or six stops, depending on reports. The overall average speed was 63mph, but one lengthy section was timetabled for an average start-to-stop speed of 73.9mph. The locomotives involved in running the trains were initially Atlantics, the 1 4–2 wheel

The Hiawatha 4–4–2 Atlantics were specially constructed in 1935 to haul the Milwaukee Railroad out of financial difficulties, and proved so successful that they were soon replaced by 4–6–4s to deal with resulting increased loadings. Nevertheless, they were not the last streamlined steam design to revert to a four-coupled configuration – a temptation avoided by Gresley and Stanier. (*Mitchell Library*)

arrangement first pioneered for express use on the US Eastern Seaboard in the 1890s, but succeeded by Pacifics as new construction in Britain by the early 1920s.

Interestingly, the central trunk services out of Chicago were contested by at least three railroads, two of them operating streamlined trains, one steam, one diesel. According to the railway press at the time, it seems that *all* these services – including the Chicago, Burlington & Quincy streamlined Zephyr diesel railcars, and the Chicago & North Western's unstreamlined 400 express, as well as the Hiawatha – were a commercial success. The three-coach Zephyr service had to be strengthened with an extra coach, and it is quite possible that the public razzmatazz generated extra traffic.

Just as the fast Clipper ships, such as *Cutty Sark*, which operated the tea trade in the 1870s, were Sail's last reply to Steam, so streamlined trains were Steam's last throw against the encroaching Diesel, this time on land. This was particularly true on the three aforementioned lines out of Chicago, where the Hiawatha and the 400 – accelerated in 1935 but not streamlined for another three years – were designed as cheap and fairly instant replies to the Burlington's Zephyr diesels.

A detailed study of these three services in competition with one another would be particularly interesting. There is no doubt however, of the excellence of the steam locomotive work required to compete with the new diesel services. The international rail expert Baron Vuillet quite simply credits the Hiawatha with being the 'fastest steam-hauled train that ever ran'.

Vuillet wrote in some detail about the running of this train in 1937, when it was still operated by Atlantic power. The literature recording its operation by more powerful Hudson 4–6–4s from mid-1938 until the onset of dieselisation is regrettably sparse, and accounts which do exist are liberally, and irritatingly, sprinkled with assurances that 125mph was a familiar figure for these locomotives to attain, but with no dynamometer evidence being proffered. However, Vuillet himself found himself writing his notes at 106mph during the course of an Atlantic footplate journey on the Hiawatha service, so no doubts should be harboured as to the quality of this streamlined steam-powered operation.

It appears that the 62mph average speed required for the 410 miles between Chicago and St Paul was deceptively low, and included standing time. There was a maximum of six station stops in this distance (nine miles longer than Euston–Glasgow), and these were officially timetabled for eleven minutes (and looking like a major underestimate), as well as no fewer than 58 service checks, eleven of them to less than 40mph. Including time lost for braking and reaccelerating, plus a calculated 39 minutes lost to checks (Vuillet's figures), it is no surprise that the average running speed should work out around 74mph. This would be the *daily* equivalent of LMS Pacific No 6201's one-off 70mph dash from Glasgow to London in 1936, and was equalled in the pre-war age over a comparable distance in Europe only by Germany's *Fliegende Kölner* and perhaps the LNER's down Coronation.

The four-coupled Alco-built Atlantics working this service had 7ft 0in driving wheels, 19in x 28in cylinders, 300 lb/sq in boiler pressure, and roller bearings fitted to driving, bogie, and trailing wheels. Making a footplate trip on 15 June 1937, the much-travelled Baron recorded a 340 minute net time for the distance, a running average of 72.4mph; 42.5 gallons of water were consumed per mile by the oil-fired engine, which, as already observed, easily broke three figures. Britain's Cecil J. Allen was similarly impressed, pointing out that a 28-minute timing for a 41.5 mile section on the southbound run demanded an average speed of 88.9mph between those points.

What was particularly interesting about the Hiawatha service was the way in which the nominal concept of the train was extended into points of detail. The train ran through, and, in some cases served, communities associated with Red Indian characters immortalised by Longfellow. The naming of individual cars after such characters was thus a pleasant touch, and the press conference introducing the train featured railroad staff in traditional Indian costumes. Nor was all this a failure in attracting public attention – nearly 5,000 passengers were carried by the two train sets in the first eleven days. The beaver-tail observation car was popular despite its disappointingly small windows (it was soon re-designed) but not as successful as the train's Tip Top Tap Room, a cocktail bar which became enormously popular despite having no windows at all! It too, was to be re-designed and

extended in later variants of the train. The train's outward appearance was also striking – designer Otto Kuhler continued the silver-grey from the engine's front along the roofs of engine and train, bordered by maroon, and with orange on the lower sides. Appropriate interior decor was designed by a Chicago furniture retailer, Marshall Field & Co. American transport historian Robert C. Reed summed it all up:

'For the price of a ticket, a Minneapolis housewife or a Dubuque insurance salesman could lounge more graciously than in his [or her] own Depression-era parlor back home.'

Not a bad resumé of the public relations *raison d'être* of railway streamlining, at least in the USA. One Hiawatha traveller in 1936 noted a very high proportion of women and children among the passengers. As will be shown, British streamlined expresses (certainly on the LNER) were specifically aimed at the travelling businessman and there was more emphasis on comfort than on glamour.

A comparative analysis (see below) of the costs and revenue of the three major rail expresses connecting Chicago with the Twin Cities in June and July 1935 found that the Hiawatha, combining streamlining with a reasonable passenger capacity, scored over both its steam and diesel rivals.

Obviously, the diesel railcars had far and away the lowest running costs, saving particularly in fuel and crewing (although from 1936 the footplate union insisted on a second man in the cab), and allowing a return journey to be made each day. Nevertheless, their revenue per train mile was not high, curbed by their rigid configuration, even when a fourth coach was added. (In Germany, such vehicles were soon to be run as multiple units to increase capacity.) The Hiawatha outperformed both its rivals, proving that a 'flash' appearance does have bankable qualities, but the survey did not explain why its running costs were higher than the unstreamlined 400 – one assumes that capital costs were not included in the above,

Railroad	Train	Motive power	Whether streamlined	Cost*	Revenue*
Chicago & North Western	400	Steam	No	1.151	1.8
Chicago, Burlington & Quincy	Zephyr	Diesel	Yes	0.452	1.178
Chicago, Milwaukee, St Paul & Pacific	Hiawatha	Steam	Yes	1.189	3.659

* $ per train mile

since those of the Zephyrs would obviously be higher than those of a steam-powered service utilising everyday stock. Equally, such intangible costs as training staff to drive and maintain diesel railcars were probably not taken into account.

Streamlined trains were invariably the child of unwelcome competition. Norristown commuters enjoyed streamlined electric trains because of the efficiency of services on a rival neighbouring line; the Hiawatha and 400 were a quick and cheap answer to the Zephyrs. Cheapness was an important factor in the Milwaukee's case; according to one historian, the line had apparently

not declared a dividend since 1917, and in 1932 had lost half a million dollars. The rival Zephyrs were regarded by the railway community as being particularly expensive to design and construct, one report suggesting an original purchase cost of the equivalent of £70,000, making alternative steam services very viable initially until such costs came down.

The rival Rock Island line, deep in its third year of bankruptcy, announced in the autumn of 1936 that it was to introduce six streamlined trains, known as Rockets, on four different routes. It was an interesting illustration of how streamline trains could act as a tonic to a rail concern,

both financially and in terms of staff morale. The Rock Island made a dramatic turnaround by the end of the decade, although the Rockets were diesel-powered, obtained by special 'hire purchase'-like arrangements.

Incidentally, just as unstreamlined steam services could operate in the shadow of the *Fliegende Hamburger* to

Streamlining Belgian-style. Atlantic No 12.001 poses at Fives depot, Lille, in July 1956, showing its striking combination of a streamlined front *and* smoke deflectors, the latter carried down almost to rail level, with cutaways for ease of maintenance. These Atlantics were still operating in the 1960s. (*W. E. Boyd*)

within a few minutes of the much-vaunted diesel, so had steam services to substitute for the Zephyr diesel when public demand for seats could not be catered for with a three-coach unit, even when augmented. It was reported at the time that steam could keep within five minutes of the diesel schedule in the eastbound direction, although there was a more serious time loss westbound (presumably in the face of adverse gradients). The pressure on the Hiawatha, caused by its success, was answered simply by running more than one section, each carrying up to 380 passengers. One report records that up to seven sections were run daily, and, as we have seen, the Milwaukee line introduced larger streamlined steam engines to power their later streamlined services, just as the French did.

When one considers how the Zephyr had cut scheduled times between the Lakes and the Plains of the USA, it is perfectly obvious that steam power could have been accelerated years before had the will been there to do so. In other words, the previous best steam-hauled times were not necessarily the fastest that could be attained before the advent of diesels; it took road and air competition to force railway managements in the central USA – to say nothing of Britain – to provide a faster, and therefore better, public service.

The autumn of 1935 saw the introduction of streamlined steam services in Britain, but it should not blind us to a parallel event taking place in France, even if it means breaking the chronological narrative once again before turning to British railway streamlining. Interestingly, not only did the PLM (Paris–Lyons–Mediterranean) railway introduce a streamlined steam train set into service, but it did so in the same timetable with Bugatti diesel railcars. An added dash of interest lay in the age of the locomotive – 28-year-old Atlantic No 221.A14.

Early in 1936 British transport journalists were given the opportunity of a footplate trip on the PLM streamliner and their accounts made interesting reading. The engine locomotive had 78.7in driving wheels and a boiler pressure of 232 lb/sq in. It sported a bulbous apron-like

streamline casing not a million miles removed from that later to be adopted by Stanier on the LMS, except for a more obtrusive chimney design. With a specially constructed three-coach train, soon complemented by a fourth vehicle incorporating restaurant and baggage facilities, the veteran Atlantic would certainly appear to offer a more commodious alternative to its modern Bugatti rivals operating on the same services.

Over the 317.3 miles between Paris (Gare de Lyon) and Lyons, both diesel and steam-powered *rapides* were allowed 289 minutes down and one minute more up, this with two stops. The steam service took water at Dijon, giving it a running average speed of 61.4mph. Incidentally, the locomotive tender capacity of 6,600 gallons of water, and 6.75 tons of coal, was roofed over, water being taken through one of three apertures with lever-operated lids. Apparently the Atlantic had to observe a 75mph limit, although 96mph had been reached on test on 12 July 1935. One trial had pitted the streamlined Atlantic against an unstreamlined but modernised sister hauling a similar load, and it was found that around 450hp was saved by the streamlined locomotive when heading four coaches at 87mph. William Stanier of the LMS reported in 1936 that these tests had proved that streamlining could save up to 28 per cent in coal consumption, and 23 per cent in water, something obviously of considerable interest to him as he planned a streamlined service over a 400 mile distance. His former railway, the Great Western, saw little need for such economy over distances of around 120 miles, as we shall see.

Eight of the PLM Atlantics were streamlined, proving so successful that they supplanted the Bugattis altogether on this service, according to some sources, and extended their range to a nine hour Paris–Marseilles service, before themselves being replaced by Pacifics. In 1939 European streamlining came to an inevitable halt, but not before neighbouring Belgium had entered the Streamline Age.

*   *   *

Belgium was slow to join the streamline craze and found its first services virtually stillborn by the onset of World War II. On 15 May 1939 – six years to the day since the *Fliegende Hamburger* first ran – streamlined rail services were introduced to link Brussels with Ostend (70.8 miles) in one hour exactly, inclusive of a 60-second stop at Bruges. The Brussels to Bruges section, comprising 57.7 miles in 46 minutes, required an average speed of 75.3mph start-to-stop, one of the fastest in the world by any kind of traction.

Once again it was steam which accomplished this feat. A class of six Atlantics was specially introduced, complete with the kind of 'baby whale' vertical streamlining already seen on the LMS by then, except that, quite unusually, huge smoke deflectors were fitted, and there were cutaways over the cylinders and driving wheels. With driving wheels only 1.37in less than 7ft, and weighing in at 163 tons tare, the 4–4–2s were to prove one of the most distinctive streamlined designs in the world, and were still in service as late as 1962, although in ordinary passenger traffic. One is preserved, and its need for smoke deflectors is an interesting contrast to the LNER's A4 where, as we shall see, the need to remove smoke from the driver's vision was from the first an integral part of the streamline design.

The success of the substitute steam services in both the USA and Germany, not forgetting the C&NW's 400, raises the question if it was strictly necessary at that time to re-equip with diesel in the first place, when a modern steam unit could do the job without staff re-training or high initial capital expense. Compare the research and development hiatus between the outshopping of the *Fliegende Hamburger* in 1932 and its entering service fourteen months later, with that of the Silver Jubilee which was running within seven months of its announcement, never mind actual building. But there is even a supplementary question as to whether *streamlined* steam operation was necessary at all, certainly over comparatively short distances, a question which Britain's Great Western Railway was to raise.

3 GWR – 'GREAT WITHOUT RESTYLING'

Since 1933 the GWR had been timetabling its Cheltenham Flyer up from Swindon to Paddington at high speed (77.3 miles in 65 minutes). One particular journey in the previous year was accomplished at an average speed of 81.68mph and was regarded as the acme of international steam operation at the time. Of course, the 'Flyer' was not offering a terminus-to-terminus service at high speed (its overall speed was actually 52.1mph between London and Cheltenham), nor was the distance involved quite in the Dalian–Hsingking or Chicago St Paul category, but it was a sterling feat nevertheless.

At the beginning of September 1935, ostensibly to mark the centenary of the GWR's foundation, but also neatly stealing the LNER's thunder (the Silver Jubilee was due to begin running on the 30th of the month), the Great Western introduced a new service known as the Bristolian. Here, in 'the streamlined age', was the management of a major railway company scheduling an express to travel 118 miles in 105 minutes, including nearly 70 miles to be accomplished at 80mph, with no allowances made to overcoming the problems of air resistance. Neither locomotive nor train would be streamlined – the former was likely to be at least seven years old – and the trial run between London and Bristol took place only three weeks before the service was due to start. The down journey was routed via Bath and required an average speed of 67.6mph, while the return journey via Badminton required 67.2mph, including the Swindon–Southall dash, mentioned above, at 79.5mph for 68.2 miles.

The trial train comprised seven coaches of 265 tons gross, hauled by King class 4-6-0 No 6000 *King George V*, the run being accomplished in the up direction only, some 29 seconds over timetable, possibly due to an over-cautious approach into the Paddington platform. The first service on 9 September – three weeks before the début

of the Jubilee – was accomplished punctually in the down direction by the same locomotive. Although unstreamlined, the GWR engines had no difficulty in maintaining a schedule demanding a slightly higher overall average speed than that of the Silver Jubilee's. The Bristolian was early on six of its first nine down journeys, and late three times, although the worst of its three slightly unpunctual runs was due to permanent way work. Coming up to London on the first nine occasions, the express was punctual five times, early thrice, and incurred a total lateness of exactly half a minute in nine days! On the following 24 February, a fine individual run took place, when Driver Street wielded the regulator of No 6001 *King Edward VII* to such effect that an eight-minute late departure from Bristol (Temple Meads) was all but made up by Paddington, reached in only 98 minutes for the 117.6 miles.

Curiously, the GWR was experimenting with locomotive streamlining, but not exactly in a wholehearted way; in view of the successful introduction of the Bristolian, why trouble with streamlining at all? The short distances covered by most GWR journeys would render unlikely one of the strongest operational reasons for streamlining – the saving of fuel over, say, 350 miles, which might be critical in relation to the coal capacity of the average locomotive tender. There was obviously no chance of a King or a Castle running out of coal between London and Bristol, or on the Cheltenham Flyer, so one wonders why the company experimented with streamlining, if not purely for publicity reasons.

This tinkering, for that is what it amounted to, consisted of a bulbous proboscis being mounted on the locomotive's smokebox door, 'fins' being extended behind the chimney and brass safety valve cover, coverings on the forward edges of the outside cylinders, a wedge-shaped extension to the cab, and one long straight splasher each side, for which new nameplates were

made. King class No 6014 *King Henry VII* was the first Swindon engine to be treated in this way, early in 1935, to be followed by Castle Class No 5005 *Manorbier Castle* (already responsible for a 77mph dash from Paddington to Swindon, without any cosmetic 'air-smoothing'). French-born Raymond Loewy, one of the pioneers of streamlining in the USA, described this semi-metamorphosis as 'quite attractive' with 'aesthetic possibilities'. GWR admirers are not likely to agree with him!

How these locomotives came to have this style of streamlining is the subject of a much-repeated story which challenges credibility. Apparently Charles B. Collett, the line's chief mechanical engineer since 1921, received a Board directive early in 1935 to take the GWR into the streamline age, and to do so preferably before the LNER. Collett, if the tale is to be believed, promptly sent for some children's plasticine and, working with a paperweight model of a King 4-6-0, added the additional 'streamlining' with his own hand, promptly sending the finished model off to the drawing office to be copied.

The inference is that the company's locomotive staff regarded streamlining as no more than an American fad, although it would surely not have been impossible to ask the Board and senior management to postpone any decision on the necessity for streamlining until the new Bristolian was in service. As it was, the somewhat cheapskate partial streamlining (which was soon reduced round the cylinder areas to prevent overheating) was strangely un-Swindon-like. It lacked the locomotive department's usual combination of professionalism and flair.

Ten years before Collett supposedly daubed plasticine on his paperweight, a freelance engineer and author named Chapman Dendy Marshall wrote a monograph entitled *The Resistance of Express Trains*. It is a slim but highly detailed analysis of air and rail resistance on railed vehicles, commenting particularly that the new science of aeronautics had created a demand for, and had

improved, wind tunnel technology, to the ultimate benefit of the railway industry. Page 58 of Marshall's monograph has a most interesting illustration. It is a line drawing of a domed smokebox door, a design which the author had originated and sent to C. J. Bowen Cooke of the former London & North Western Railway during the latter's incumbency at Crewe between 1909 and 1920. Apart from a slight difference in scale it is exactly what adorned *King Henry VII* ten years later. Not only that, but Dendy Marshall suggested the 'doming' of outside cylinders and the extension of splashers to run along to the cab in what he called 'Worsdell' style (presumably like the pre-Grouping North Eastern Railway M and R class 4–4–0s). He did not go so far as to suggest 'fins' for the chimney and top feed arrangements, although he remarked that there seemed to be no practical reason why the piping into, and from, the latter feature could not be arranged fore and aft rather than bilaterally on each side.

The monograph was published in book form by the magazine *Railway Engineering*, after appearing as a series of articles, and Marshall's work was widely reviewed by other magazines associated with the railway industry. The *Railway Gazette* predicted that it would 'provide plenty of food for thought, and as the author hopes, will further stimulate further experiment and research'. It seems unlikely that Collett or his staff were unaware of these ideas – although that would not prevent the chief mechanical engineer approaching the streamlining project

in the apparently casual way he did. Around 1932, research at the National Physical Laboratory, Teddington, sponsored by the LMS, featured a model of a Royal Scot with a bulbous smokebox extension, not unlike Marshall's seminal design. The provenance of the GWR streamlining programme, if it can be called that, is perhaps worthy of reappraisal.

O. S. Nock has argued that Collett should have taken the matter more seriously and designed a complete streamlined casing. Whether there was any real operational basis for such an argument – given the exemplary standard of the company's existing passenger services – is doubtful. In 1936 the unstreamlined No 6027 *King Richard I*, driven by Driver Field, headed the down Bristolian into the teeth of a gale, gaining over a minute on schedule, despite a signal check, and with 90 miles run at not less than 70mph. Unless fuel consumption became a critical factor in the equation – and it obviously was not, over this kind of distance – it is difficult to imagine how this kind of performance could be bettered by other steam units.

Not surprisingly, within eight months No 6014 had lost part of its cylinder skirting and its tender cowling, its other fittings surviving until 1943, apart from the wedge-fronted cab and special snifting valves which lasted until June 1953. The Castle kept its frontal coverings and tender cowling until May 1937, and its bullnose to March 1939. The chimney and safety valve cowlings lasted until 1943,

the straight splashers and adapted cab until 1946, but the engine was withdrawn in February 1960 with only the special type of snifting valve as evidence of its flirtation with the passing enthusiasm for streamlining.

It is, however, perhaps a measure of the public relations value of streamlining that, if asked which famous British express with a high speed schedule was introduced in September 1935, the majority of railway enthusiasts might well remember the Silver Jubilee rather than the Bristolian. But this would surely leave Swindon admirers unmoved; after all, what did GWR mean if not 'Great Without Restyling'?

* * *

The Southern Railway also tentatively addressed the concept of streamlining. Schools class 4–4–0 No 935 *Sevenoaks* received a wooden 'shell' mock-up in 1939, courtesy of Oliver Bulleid, the assembly being described by one writer as a 'curious kind of inverse scalloping'. *Sevenoaks* did not enter service in this garb, to which smoke deflectors were added after the initial fitting-out, and Sean Day-Lewis has commented cleverly that the alteration of the locomotive's number to 999 suggested that 'murder had been done'. If nothing else, this interesting snippet of locomotive lore proved that *all* the British 'big four' companies experimented with streamlining, to a greater or lesser degree.

'Quite attractive, with aesthetic possibilities'. Great Western aficionados are unlikely to agree with French-born designer Raymond Loewy's verdict on GWR Castle class 4–6–0 No 5005 *Manorbier Castle* when 'streamlined' in 1935. As revealed in the text, new historical research has suggested that a 1919 design by Chapman Dendy Marshall may have inspired the GWR's chief mechanical engineer, C. B. Collett, to produce what was probably never a serious attempt at streamlining. (*Millbrook House*)

4 LNER – FROM FLYING SCOTSMAN TO SILVER JUBILEE

It was against this international background of a craze for transport streamlining that the LNER decided in 1934 to investigate the prospect of operating its own high speed service between London and industrial cities in the North of England.

While the company was undoubtedly preparing for its own contribution to the world of speed, this would hardly be discernible judging from public remarks made by the company's chairman, William Whitelaw, on 12 November 1934. Less than three weeks before a high speed express trial run was made between London and Leeds, Whitelaw informed a meeting of the Institute of Transport that the LNER system was unsuited to high speed exploits, as it was 'honeycombed with underground workings'. Either the chairman was keeping his company's cards very close to his chest, or nobody at the LNER told the chairman anything! On 8 March the following year he was promising a streamlined London–Newcastle service, to be called the Silver Jubilee. In the interval between these two public pronouncements, the LNER Board and management had learned from practical experience that their locomotives could run fast, as well as pull hard.

Surprisingly – in view of the high reputation for operational efficiency that Gresley's Pacifics already enjoyed – genuine consideration was given to introducing diesel railcars to the East Coast main line.

The advantages of operating self-contained railcars as against locomotive-hauled expresses were their lower running costs, and, with their lighter weights, their ability to accelerate impressively. Against this, were ranged their

high purchase cost, the obviously greater adaptability of locomotives, allowing for an increase in the length of a train, its passenger accommodation and catering facilities, and the ability of the locomotive to operate other services. Diesel railcars could overcome this criticism of their limited configuration to a certain extent by allowing multiple-unit working, which the Germans began to do from 1936. With no corridor running throughout the entire train, unnecessary duplication of guard accommodation and catering facilities resulted, in vehicles where a streamlined appearance precluded frontal corridor connections. As for their inability to operate other types of service, such as freight, there was no way at all around this disadvantage for a railcar; it could, however, offer greater availability through cutting preparation time. Incidentally, by 1936 American operators were beginning to examine the diesel locomotive as a more adaptable alternative to railcars of similar power, but apparently this was not considered by the LNER at the time, suggesting that German experience, rather than American, was seen as more relevant to British conditions.

First of all, could steam power come near to equalling diesel railcar speeds with a light load? The question was surely worth asking, given how firmly locked into steam traction Britain's railways were, with the obvious bonuses of ensured fuel supplies (ie coal), no reliance on imported equipment, and a minimum of staff re-training.

There was only one way for the LNER to find out steam's potential for speed, and that was to give a Gresley Pacific its head with a lightweight train. In Germany at that very time, a streamlined 4–6–4 was in the process of being constructed and tested as an alternative to diesel propulsion, but it is significant that instead of trying out a streamlined steam prototype the LNER thought it necessary to see if a whole *train* could be run fast. It was a tacit admission that the company's existing services had no such pretension, despite the fact that the LNER had

Gresley's Pacifics and no fewer than four pre-Grouping studs of Atlantic 4–4–2s, three of them acknowledged as free-running machines, available since 1923. This point was not to go unnoticed by the company's critics, as we shall see. At the same time, a trial was necessary to see what practical effects a fast train would have on other traffic – on a system where there were so many slow-moving freight trains.

The latter point was seen as crucial by LNER staff. Writing later, after the successful introduction of streamlined services, Sir Nigel Gresley commented on the difficulties of operating high-speed trains through Britain's rail network where there were 1½ million wagons running without brakes which could be operated from the locomotive. Obviously this meant that goods train speeds had to be kept low. As has been mentioned, a post-war study found that the average British goods train averaged only seven mph. To make matters even more complicated, nearly half of that number of wagons were privately owned by the railways' customers. To convert these, assuming that the owners' co-operation were to be obtained, would cost £30 million at 1936 prices.

On 30 November 1934, the first of two high-speed trials was held on the LNER main line out of King's Cross. Streamlined Pacifics might be steaming across the wilds of Manchuria with specially-built coaches and an observation car, but the LNER was not going to do anything similar without trial and experiment. When asked for information and putative timings (for a three-car 115 ton, 2 × 410hp railcar seating 140, in unavoidably cramped conditions), the German makers of the *Fliegende Hamburger*, Wagen und Maschinenbau AG, had advised the LNER that a 165 minute schedule between King's Cross and Leeds was practicable, comprising 116 minutes, plus a provisional ten per cent reserve, over the 155 miles to Doncaster and 34 minutes (plus three minutes) from there on to Leeds.

LNER expresses, pre-1935, invariably looked like this – long, heavy, and only occasionally well-loaded. A3 No 2750 *Papyrus*, which showed in 1935 what it could do in the way of running a light express between London and Newcastle in less than four hours, here is heading the down Flying Scotsman at Sandy on 9 June 1933.
(*National Railway Museum*)

The object was to see if an ordinary Pacific, with 44,176 miles since its last heavy repair, could take a four-coach train over the 185 miles from London to Leeds in 165 minutes. One of the four vehicles was a dynamometer car, the train's passenger capacity, assuming four ordinary coaches, being equal to 156 seats, 50 per cent more than the *Fliegende Hamburger*. The locomotive was none other than No 4472 *Flying Scotsman*, not universally regarded as King's Cross' best, but a favourite for any public relations exercises such as the first run of the northbound Flying Scotsman express when it resumed its non-stop schedule each summer. The crew comprised Driver Sparshatt and Fireman Webster.

When the guard's whistle blew, No 4472, as described by F. A. S. Brown, invoked Lady Macbeth's words to her husband 'Stand not upon the order of your going, but go at once'. Bursting out from the main suburban platform at King's Cross terminus, the Pacific was up to 'even time' by Brookman's Park, and had bettered the schedule by 5½ minutes to Peterborough, passed 39 seconds over the even hour. Eighty mph was the minimum in climbing Stoke Bank, the summit 100.1 miles from London, being passed in 79.5 minutes. Leeds (Central) was reached 13 minutes early in just under 152 minutes at an average speed of 73.4mph.

It was a triumphant vindication of steam power's ability to haul light loads at speed, and a tribute to the professionalism of the footplate staff, who could scarcely be described as being specially trained for this kind of all-or-nothing dash. For the return journey, two coaches were added to bring the total stock up to six, and the engine-drawbar apparatus was tightened to prevent oscillations at speed, as had been experienced on the down journey. Despite this precaution, these were again evidenced on the resulting run but Wedgwood assured the Board that '[At] two or three places . . . slight shocks were experienced due to the track . . . but the [civil] Engineer can readily rectify matters and has already taken action'.

The return journey was accomplished in 157 minutes and 17 seconds, arriving nearly eight minutes early at an average speed of nearly 71mph. This would have been even faster had Fireman Webster not been understandably tired, but *Flying Scotsman* was timed by Cecil J. Allen as running 3.5 miles down Stoke Bank at an average of 97.3mph, and 15.2 miles at just over 90mph. This section of the run included an acknowledged '100', since subsequently queried by O. S. Nock in his book *Speed Records on British Railways*, although it scarcely matters now. Nor

did it then, being topped within a few months on the same section of line by the same driver, while the company's officials would be more pleased with the high speeds up the bank rather than down, and it was calculated that the journey between the capital city and Yorkshire had included no fewer than 250 miles run at an average of 80mph or more. All this was achieved by an unstreamlined 13-year-old machine with a 180 lb/sq in pressure boiler.

Three days into 1935, chief general manager Ralph Wedgwood circulated a memorandum to the board of directors summarising the lessons learned from the *Flying Scotsman* trial, as well as from a visit to Germany by LNER staff the previous autumn. The conclusions drawn from the latter seemed to strengthen the suspicion that the 'exceptionally favourable' permanent way played a major part in the success of the *Fliegende Hamburger*, prompting Wedgwood to make the following observation:

'the [diesel] engine did not appear to have much margin of haulage or accelerating power. It was felt that the heavy grades, speed restrictions, and greater density of traffic in this country would make the maintenance of similar speeds impracticable.'

A second trial was arranged for 5 March 1935, this time over the 268 mile King's Cross–Newcastle stretch. The load was six coaches of 213 tons tare to be hauled by Class A3 No 2750 *Papyrus*. Driver Gutteridge was in charge northwards, to be relieved by Sparshatt on the return journey, thus ensuring a fresh crew to take advantage of the fast stretches when approaching the capital.

The northbound running was more restrained than that of *Flying Scotsman*, although still very creditable – less than 88 minutes for the 105 miles to Grantham. At Doncaster, the 'trialist' had to negotiate its way round a derailed freight, and York was passed one minute late. Nevertheless, Newcastle was reached (despite those underground workings warned of by Whitelaw!), in three minutes less than the four hours allowed for the journey.

After the disappointing end to the return journey on the previous trial, it was interesting to see what a fresh crew could do. The early part of the southward run was comparatively unremarkable, and the emergency workings in the Doncaster area still had their effect, but south of that point, the A3 really ran. Stoke summit was topped

at 69mph and the speed pushed into three figures, giving the LNER a British record that no one could dispute.

Three hundred miles were covered at an average of 80mph and 12.3 miles at 100.6mph. This had included a new maximum of 108mph – a British record for an unstreamlined steam engine not equalled until well into the 1950s and never beaten. In recent years the *Gresley Observer*, the magazine of the Gresley Society, has published a detailed technical analysis of this run (see the Bibliography) and its author speculates that *Papyrus* was eased at milepost 91 when the maximum occurred; an even higher total would not apparently have been a problem. Water had been collected at the five sets of troughs at very high speed, above 80mph on three occasions, a velocity usually sufficient to considerably shorten the working life of the engine's scoop. No 2750 had accumulated nearly 400,000 miles in its working life since 1928, and 7,719 since last overhaul. The day after that record run No 2750 was rostered to the 5.30pm ex-King's Cross, one of the most important down trains in the timetable, proving that its high-speed dash had not caused any ill-effects to an engine which was to be immortalised in a book *2750: Legend of a Locomotive* in post-war years.

Perhaps the only slight cause for concern about the trial run of 5 March was the reported coal consumption of 43 lb/mile – nevertheless an improvement on *Flying Scotsman*'s trial run the previous November, when 54 lb/mile had been consumed with a lighter load. Both rates were higher than on heavy long-distance runs, so if high-speed trains were to be considered for, say, the London–Edinburgh run at some future time, a 9 ton tender would be required to allow a sufficient reserve, particularly if an all year round service was considered, when adverse winds would have to be taken into account. This is a point that will be returned to later.

The achievement of *Papyrus* reflected great credit on the LNER's CME, his staff, and the running department. As a team they had bettered by 18 minutes down and 23 minutes up the 255 minutes schedule postulated for the 268 miles by German diesel experts, and with nearly twice the passenger capacity, even allowing for full restaurant facilities. Not only that, but the delay caused by the Doncaster derailment on this occasion acted as makeweight for a possible stop in a four-hour timetable.

'What might have been achieved in the way of speed with such special preparations as streamlining, or roller bearings for engines and coaches, and modern French front-end design, such as has been applied to the new LNER 2–8–2 locomotive *Cock o' the North*, staggers the imagination.'

So wrote the *Railway Gazette* in March 1935 commenting on the run of *Papyrus*, although not all of the reaction in that magazine was as positive. One letter writer to the editor demanded to know, on learning that No 2750 was nearly seven years old, why this kind of performance could not have been made much earlier and an accelerated express service put into effect as a result. He received no reply from the LNER.

*   *   *

Air transport was seen as a coming threat to long-distance rail services in Britain, although this threat was more imaginary than real in the 1930s. Unfortunately, with streamlining very much a product of the imagination anyway, even an illusory threat of competition from the air must have seemed real enough to railway managers, so it should not be ignored in this history. In 1936 for example, the assistant general manager of the LNER informed the Institute of Transport that 'air transport within Great Britain has so far been too spasmodic seriously to menace railway traffics' – this, six months after the introduction of the nation's first streamlined train. Nevertheless, it could be argued that its introduction was in the manner of pre-empting competition from the air, which railway managers were aware of, and to a certain extent, overestimated.

On 20 August 1934 the first Anglo-Scottish air service began when two de Havilland 86s took off from Renfrew airfield near Glasgow for Belfast. This was the first stage of a 4¼ hour flight to Croydon via Belfast, Manchester and Birmingham. Ironically, on a day of gale-force winds the scheduled flight had to be abandoned at Manchester, with the mail having to be sent south by train; one of the planes could only proceed to the capital when conditions had improved. In fact eight of the first 70 journeys on this pioneer route operated by Railway Air Services (RAS) were abandoned – not a bad performance considering the difficulties, not to mention dangers, involved, but hardly a reassuring record of service. There would be no question of one in nine long-distance express trains being abandoned en route in the 1930s!

City centre to city centre, RAS was offering a 5½ hour service between London and Glasgow, and the historian might see this as a spur to induce the railways to invest in new express train technology and rolling stock. In fact, the four main lines invested in RAS, as the name implies, the parallel investment in streamlined services being perhaps less lavish than it might have been, as will become evident, although the capacity of the aircraft, ten passengers, was hardly likely to give rail management sleepless nights at this time. Indeed, on the Glasgow to Renfrew road leg of the journey, a car was sufficient to ferry passengers from the Central Station to the airfield. Air travel in Britain before World War II was not so much an innovation as a gimmick. In his history of the subject, John Stroud comments that empty seats on the de Havilland aircraft were a common sight.

London–Newcastle air services were introduced by North Eastern Airways around this time, but were withdrawn from July 1935, although whether this was due to publicity for the then-forthcoming Silver Jubilee is not known. More probable is the fact that rail and air services operated in a complete vacuum from each other at the time. NEA appears to have re-commenced operations between Croydon, Newcastle and Perth, in November 1936, when the LNER was performing very well on the London–Newcastle corridor. Again, air travel appears to have had more of a psychological impact on rail managers than a material effect on revenue, generating fear of losing traffic while inspiring new outlines for rail vehicles; after all, the wind tunnel which decided the shape of the A4 and the LMS Princess Coronation was very much a tool of the aeronautics industry.

Nevertheless, while air travel offered an elitist means of travel, the railways had one more reason to respond in a media-conscious age, and this was yet another reason for streamlined steam travel. Streamlining a train was a publicity-catching exercise, and a good enticement away from air services.

*   *   *

Preparations for a streamlined locomotive and train could not solely consist of exciting dashes from Point A to Point B with an enthusiastic crew and a shortened train packed with railway staff and enthusiasts armed with stopwatches. The LNER was a commercial concern whose board was answerable to stockholders who may well have regarded railways as having as much glamour or potential for excitement as the gas industry or sewage facilities. If Wedgwood and Gresley wished to convince their directors of the likely commercial success of a streamlined train, at a recoverable cost, they would have to produce reassuring figures on paper. They had to report to the board, who had to answer to the investors. A desire to make railroading more exciting was not enough.

Wedgwood could doubtless find figures to prove that a London–Newcastle streamliner would be profitable – there was an increase in such traffic already – but Gresley would have to reassure the LNER directors that such a service could be expedited economically. Research was needed, designed to show how fuel could be saved through employing streamlining to reduce coal consumption while producing power to overcome air resistance. In any event, Gresley was a gifted engineer and had a supplementary purpose in contemplating wind tunnel research, in attempting to find a front-end design which would lift exhaust smoke and steam over the cab. The LNER was quite capable of introducing the first streamlined train to Britain's tracks, but it could not help its driver if he failed to catch sight of a signal. There was no automatic cab signalling system on the East Coast main line until the 1960s; a perfectly workable system on the former North Eastern section had actually been dismantled.

One of the reasons why streamlining became a vogue for land transport in the early 1930s was the availability of empirical means of determining the effects of air resistance in the laboratory. This was thanks to the invention of the wind tunnel, usually ascribed to the Wright brothers experimenting a couple of years before their first powered flight in 1903.

The LNER's use of wind tunnel experiments to help with its express locomotive design appears to date from 1929, with the building of Gresley's 'Hush-Hush' 4–6–4 No 10000. Academic advice was apparently taken from Professor W. E. Dalby on the design of the front end to ensure that smoke was blown back over the roof of the cab. In later discussion, when chairing a meeting of the Institution of Mechanical Engineers, Gresley talked of using models one-twelfth full size in such wind tunnel tests, and named the City & Guilds Engineering College in London (Dalby's college at that time) as having assisted in general, although Gresley was not specific about details.

In November 1936 a paper on wind tunnel testing

to determine streamlined outlines for locomotives and rolling stock was presented by F. C. Johansen to the Institution, with Gresley in the chair. This research at the National Physical Laboratory had been commissioned by the LMS, LNER and Southern Railways, although Johansen's paper appears to have been presented as a personal interpretation of the results obtained. (He had left the NPL in 1932 to set up the LMS research facility at Derby.)

Indeed, the LNER's participation was somewhat enigmatic, since one of the paper's sternest critics was Gresley's assistant Oliver Bulleid, who in particular questioned the methodology used. He was frankly sceptical of extrapolating results from models one-fortieth size to the full scale prototype to obtain conclusions on air resistant outlines, believing this would lead to any imprecision in calculations being grossly magnified. Gresley contented himself with commenting that Johansen's conclusions were consistent with those obtained earlier by the LNER, although it is noticeable that the locomotive models used for that company's part in the research were not streamlined (despite the A4 already being in service), while both the LMS models (a Royal Scot class 4–6–0 and train) were garbed in both semi-streamlined and fully streamlined casings. Presumably the LMS was the more interested in this experiment, although the modern reader, even one not technically-minded, must wonder with Bulleid how results from a model scaled between gauges 0 and 1 could offer useful data when applied to a full-size machine.

Gresley's comment about previous test results using one-twelfth scale models to determine front end air resistance is interesting, if not downright puzzling. The NPL Annual Reports only mention one experiment commissioned by the railway companies on this subject. Indeed, the first such summary, in the 1931 report, published early in the following year, mentions only the LMS as customer. It is joined by the LNER in the following year's summary of research which was intended

'. . . to analyse the air resistance of a train by measuring the separate contribution of each vehicle, and to arrive at a limit of air resistance reduction by comparing a model train of standard design with an ideal model free from all excrescences . . . a few additional tests on one-twelfth scale model LNE models have yielded results which confirm those obtained from the smaller models'.

This was published in 1933, and appears to be exactly the same experiment reported on by Johansen over three years later. By then the LNER had been running a streamlined train service for over a year, while the LMS, which had sponsored the research in the first place, had still to produce its Coronation Scot. There is no hint anywhere in the documentation of a wedge-shaped front-end as seen on the A4, and no evidence of the more vertical rounded front shape later favoured by Stanier. Nor are these facts too surprising – Gresley had not seen the Bugatti-shaped French railcars when these experiments were begun, while Stanier had not even been appointed as CME when this NPL research project was initiated.

The 'ideal' train which was the hypothetical basis for the NPL experiments carried a streamlined shroud down to rail level with an apparent vertical wedge at the front. It was certainly not the basis for either the A4 or Princess Coronation (not least because it was apparently a 4–6–0). Incidentally, Johansen argued that streamlining down to rail level appeared necessary to ensure reduction of air resistance – 'a surprisingly large proportion of the air resistance of a coach . . . is contributed by the bogies and undercarriage structure. It is subsequently advantageous to use articulated stock'. The LNER was already doing so on its streamlined service, while the LMS, originally the commissioners of this research, did not! Johansen was, perhaps unconsciously, following in Dionysius Lardner's footsteps – the 19th-century scientist had argued that revolving wheels, acting as 'blowers', themselves set up air turbulence, and at roughly 30mph!

It is difficult to assess the significance of the LMS/LNER commissioned experiments at Teddington. Every written history of the development of Gresley's Pacifics names the NPL as being significant in being the source of the wedge-shaped prow of the A4 which was to bring Britain the Blue Riband of steam-powered rail speed. Indeed, Gresley announced in his 1936 presidential address to the Institution of Mechanical Engineers that this was the location for comparative tests between models of an A4 and an unstreamlined Pacific. In the absence of evidence specific to when the LNER commissioned this research, this author assumes that the NPL's facilities were used on a casual hire basis in 1935, something which correspondence with the Laboratory has failed to establish.

It appears that early wind tunnel experiments on the proposed A4 seemed likely to vindicate a 'straight-backed' shape, with chimney, boiler top, and cab roof in

line and at the same height. It was then noticed that the French chalk, used to simulate smoke, was certainly lifted clear of the driver's view when facing a head wind, but that this shape would not clear exhaust in a side wind. Gresley had taken advice from Professor W. E. Dalby in his design of the front end of the 'Hush-Hush' 4–6–4 in 1929, and turned again to this academic for guidance.

Dalby had rather unusually entered the groves of Academe through an engineering apprenticeship at the Stratford Works of the former Great Eastern Railway, before giving up a promising railway career at Crewe to help establish an engineering department at Cambridge University. He had served on the Bridge Stress Committee in the 1920s which established that it was a steam engine's 'hammer blow', rather than its weight, which was a crucial loading factor on bridges, a fact which was of seminal importance. Following retirement through illness in 1931, Dalby was, by the time of his work on the A4, Emeritus Professor of Engineering at London University, and his (few) obituaries do not detail his work for Gresley on smoke clearing. The fact that Gresley had to seek advice on an important design matter from an independent engineering consultant, while the rival LMS was busy setting up its own research and development centre, is something of a black mark against the LNER.

Eric Bannister was working as part of the LNER's design team and he has recorded his experiences in a useful volume of reminiscence. Apparently Gresley had delegated the detailed design of the streamlining to assistants sent to work with Dalby using the Teddington facilities, and, so resigned were they to defeat in the problem of keeping the driver's view clear through an efficient front-end design, that they were on the point of adding smoke deflectors to the model of the A4! According to Bannister:

'Professor Dalby had some stiff card available for trials (but) at first we tried the model just as it had been supplied from Doncaster and then

A splendid shot of *Silver Link* receiving attention at King's Cross after one of its earliest runs in 1935. The 'shark's jaws' have been opened by turning the key fitted into the casing just in front of the nearside cylinder, revealing the mass of ash inside the smokebox. The recessed drawgear is also visible and was soon to be extended, following a fatal accident caused by the insufficient room for a shunter when the A4 was buffered-up to another engine in the depot. (*P. Ransome-Wallis/National Railway Museum*)

lifted it out. When it was on the table, we noticed a depression in the plasticine fairing behind the chimney, apparently made by one of us when we had lifted out the model from the wind tunnel.'

On an impulse Dalby and Bannister tried the model with the accidental thumbprint left exactly as it was – and found that the French chalk was deflected well clear of the cab. They repeated the test, and then applied their calculations accordingly.

In other words, it appears that a careless handling of plasticine determined the final appearance of the A4. Shades of Collett's paperweight! Suffice to say that the A4 was designed with the driver's needs nicely balanced with the aesthetics of the design. As we shall see, the LMS wind tunnel researchers were less fastidious in this respect, and both German and Belgian examples of streamlining incorporated smoke deflectors into the front-end design.

The timescale of all this was impressive. On 25 October 1935, with the Silver Jubilee having completed its first highly successful month, Gresley wrote to Wedgwood with a summary of what had been achieved. It can be summarised as follows:

High Speed Trial run with No 2750		5 March
'Outline diagram of suggested train' submitted to Wedgwood		11 March
(Day Zero) Approved by Board. Drawings ordered		28 March
(Day 50) A4 cylinder drawings submitted to Gresley		17 May
(Day 60) Carriage underframes from York to Doncaster		27 May
(Day 70) Outside cylinders cast at Gorton		6 June
(Day 71) Inside cylinder cast at Doncaster		7 June
(Day 90) Engine frames laid down		26 June
(Day 163) Engine steamed for first time		7 September
(Day 173) Train completed		17 September
(Day 186) Entered service		30 September

It was an extraordinary *tour de force* of industrial organisation involving three different manufacturing centres, plus laboratory tests at a fourth, and a confident intrusion into a world of high speed transport engineering with little or no existing expertise to call on.

* * *

While the Jubilee's rolling-stock could be described as disappointingly traditional in construction and character – a point more fully considered later in this chapter and in the Postscript – the same could not be said about the train's locomotive, the first A4 Pacific No 2509 *Silver Link*. Although in many ways a logical extension of the lines along which Nigel Gresley had been working with his A1s and A3s, and in many respects less innovatory than his 'Hush-Hush' 4–6–4, or the P2 2–8–2s, nevertheless it is fascinating to savour the impact that the new streamlined engines had on the British railway community.

It is surely unnecessary for the A4 to be described to the reader; this author will assume that this handsome class of locomotives is well known enough for him to look instead at the effect of its introduction on the technical expert and layman alike.

In his biography of Sir Nigel Gresley, F. A. S. Brown admits to having been shocked when he first saw a picture of No 2509 in a newspaper he casually picked up in an East Anglian pub. One newspaper reporter described the new Pacific as 'very like some mechanical monster that Mr H. G. Wells might have conceived. No ordinary funnel or boiler is visible.' The comment about the 'funnel' is ironic, since the chimney of the A4 is probably the most prominent of any British locomotive since the *Rocket*! The placing of the whistle ahead of the chimney was also

The fourth of the original A4s, No 2512 *Silver Fox*, is seen inside Gateshead shed when new. The proximity to the locomotive ahead suggests that the A4 was still fitted with the dangerous recessed drawgear at this time. (*W. Stubbs*)

highly unusual and invested the locomotive with an urgency of purpose highly appropriate to one heading a high-speed train. Overall, the locomotive was compared (by a pressman) to a World War I tank which was 'silvered over and [which] had lost its cumbersomeness'.

One can only imagine the feelings stirred amongst railwaymen, often deeply conservative in operational matters, on their first sight of this machine sheeted in steel with its tapering front end and wedge-shaped cab. Cecil J. Allen described the A4, when viewed from the side, as 'one of the most beautiful and shapely examples of locomotive streamlining that the world has ever seen'. Rival engineer William Stanier, not then knighted, called it 'an example of streamlining which might be called the best looking of the lot'. Even in the 1950s and 1960s, the sight of an A4 heading an express could bring a tingle of excitement to the watcher, and this reaction is a perfect

compliment to the skill of Gresley, as gifted a designer as
he was an engineer.

For an interesting – and relevant – American reaction
to the A4's appearance, we can turn to transport historian Robert C. Reed, who disliked its 'unfortunate roach
back appearance'. This in fact is very much a comment
from an aesthetic point of view, prompted by the oval
shape of the chimney casing (when viewed from above),
modelled, as we know from Eric Bannister, to prevent
smoke being carried to the cab windows in any wind
conditions.

Reed, author of a voluminous work on American
varieties of the breed, went on to comment particularly
on the lack of painted speed lines emanating from the
front of the engine as in so many American examples –
and which were so prominent on the later LMS streamlined Pacifics. While adjudging *Silver Link* 'striking without
being outlandish', Reed at least approved of the A4's
wedged front.

Unlike so many American or continental examples of
streamlined steam, the A4's front was designed to a
horizontal plane. This is best explained by simply comparing the wedge-like shape of the Bugatti railcars, as well as
the A4 (and Calthrope's 1865 design) with, say, the Alco
Atlantic for the Hiawatha, the Borsig 4–6–4, or the later
Stanier Princess Coronation Pacifics, all of which could be
regarded as being streamlined vertically.

Unlike many of the other examples of streamlined
steam, the A4 was air-resistant right down to its footplate.
This was no temporary patch-up; there could be no
question of this class having its outer case removed as the
streamlining even extended to the smokebox, which was
cut away at the top to accommodate the wedge front
leading smoothly up to the chimney. Similarly the footplate, forming a graceful curve back to the wedge-like cab

Not intended to haul a streamlined service, the LNER's P2
2–8–2 No 2001 *Cock o' the North* had anticipated the A4 by
incorporating streamlined steam passages, although its
wedge-like front was its first of two rebuildings, and came
later than the A4. This class was ultimately rebuilt as
rather ungainly Pacifics by Gresley's successor, Edward
Thompson.   (*RAS Marketing*)

was an integral part of the design, while the valancing over the driving-wheels could be removed (and would be permanently in wartime) without, in many admirers' eyes, spoiling the engine's promise of combining speed potential with power.

Apart from its external appearance, in which Gresley's assistant Oliver Bulleid had played a part in designing the air-smoothed footplate, and to which chief draughtsman T. A. Steel had also made an important contribution, the technical press was particularly impressed by the upgrading of the boiler pressure to 250 lb/sq in, as compared with the A3. A 43 element superheater was fitted. The cylinders were 18in diameter with 26in stroke. The internal streamlining of steam passages was a crucial consideration, showing Chapelon's influence, and preventing any major drop in steam pressure between regulator and steamchest. For a detailed technical description, the reader is directed to Volume 2A of *The Locomotives of the LNER* published by the Railway Correspondence and Travel Society (RCTS).

The point about streamlined steam passages was emphasised in a run recorded by Cecil J. Allen some eleven months into the life of the new locomotive. He noted that the boiler had more than enough steam for the job in hand – the northbound Silver Jubilee – including the extra weight of the dynamometer car, and deduced that the proportions of the steam passages prevented any major drop in the pressure between the boiler and the cylinders, when anything up to 15 per cent pressure would normally be lost.

In other words, the A4 was streamlined internally as well as having a wedge-shaped prow. The angle of the latter, incidentally, was inaccurately draughted; the radius was 12ft instead of 14ft, an error missed by Gresley, according to the RCTS history. The wedge design was, as we have seen, believed to be based on the shape of the Bugatti railcars in France, Gresley being particularly impressed by the way they pushed air *upwards* when deflecting it. He had noted that a handkerchief would not deviate in its fall if dropped as a Bugatti flashed by; obviously, he could infer that the air displaced upwards would usefully lift a steam engine's smoke clear of the driver's vision, as indeed it did.

This was of crucial importance. To the modern rail driver, the outlook from a steam locomotive's cab, behind some 35ft of boiler, must seem limited enough for the crew without the added problem of steam and smoke drifting down from the chimney. But matters were

even worse: the signals to be sighted were mainly semaphores, whose lights at night were dim compared to present-day colour-lights. Indeed, throughout the modernisation of railway signalling over the last half-century, a perennial problem has been the 'over-riding' of nearby semaphores by colour-light signals at a greater distance but having greater visibility. To make matters worse, at the time that the LNER was planning to introduce streamlined trains, the East Coast main line had just had its cab signalling system *dismantled*.

From 1895 to 1933 parts of the former North Eastern line between York and Berwick had been equipped with a mechanical system invented by Sir Vincent Raven to confirm signal readings to the train driver. This was achieved by a simple trigger between the rails, activated when the distant was 'on', catching a special fitting under the engine and setting off an audible warning in the cab. It was designed as a fog warning aid, but was obviously equally useful at night, and would have had added value for high-speed trains. It seems a thousand pities that the system was not extended beyond two comparatively short stretches north of York.

As the system grew older, trouble resulted from jammed apparatus under the engine fouling other track

fittings, but its refinement and extension should have been considered. An electrical version was introduced after World War II, known as automatic train control and later, more accurately, as automatic warning system, but no streamlined train driver had the benefit of any kind of cab signalling system. If he failed to glimpse a distant because its light was out, or because of drifting exhaust from another engine, he had no option but to brake, unless he was satisfied that the subsequent home signal was 'off'. In these circumstances, Gresley's determination to remove the problem of drifting steam from the driver's view can be seen as a worthwhile priority.

Unfortunately, it was not only the question of sighting signals that was to challenge the expertise of the LNER's top footplate crews. Equally problematic was the whole new experience of running at unprecedented speeds, where even a familiar view ahead could be transformed into a bewildering succession of signals, points, and overbridges, with smoke and steam from passing trains as

Blue *Silver Link* on the Silver Jubilee. Pioneer A4 Pacific No 2509 heads the up train near Durham in the summer of 1938, after the stock had been increased to eight coaches to meet demand. *(RAS Marketing)*

an added diversion. Take for sample Driver George Haygreen's account of high speed driving down Stoke Bank in 1936:

'We averaged 108mph for six miles, and the signal posts we passed seemed as if they were jumping up and down, and you dared not put your head out of the cab window. I could also feel a pressure building up under the cab floor.'

This driver was not a nervous newcomer to railway work, but a veteran of 40 years' service. Yet his account of this trip – with fare-paying passengers in the train behind – as told later to J. M. Craig, could be mistaken for one written by a casual visitor to the footplate. The fact was that even experienced top link footplatemen had little or no experience of speeds above 90mph, particularly among former NER and NBR men, yet they were being asked to adapt to unheard-of schedules and even record speed attempts without proper training, and towards the end of their careers. The LNER compounded the error of not providing special training in the case of the later West Riding Limited. As will be seen in a subsequent chapter, the job of operating this 1937 streamlined service was given to a link of comparatively inexperienced crewmen.

What training could have been given? Would it have been unreasonable to expect the LNER in the 1930s to have produced a primitive but effective version of simulation equipment that present-day aircraft pilots use to gain experience of flight-deck conditions? The cinematic technology would have been available. But at the same time it should have been possible to run crew training specials on Sundays, with the corridor tender used to introduce crewmen to the footplate before or during passages of high-speed running. Not only was it essential for the drivers to be able to concentrate on the road ahead while signals and lineside features flashed past as in a speeded-up Mack Sennett comedy, but they were expected to observe speed restrictions – and the new A4s would carry 'Tachograph'-type equipment, known as Flaman speed recorders, to ensure that they could be disciplined if they did not do so. Yet the recorders giving a speed indication were under the *fireman's* seat, hardly much of an aid to a driver whose engine was approaching a speed ceiling! Steaming a locomotive was of course still dependent on human toil, and the fireman's place in all this will be examined later. What all this boiled down to was that the same attention was not being paid to crew

training and acclimatisation, as to the new locomotives and various technical improvements being introduced.

* * *

Order 646 for the Silver Jubilee rolling stock was placed as late as February 1935 for two articulated twin vehicles and a restaurant/kitchen car triplet. Additional accommodation was inserted in the form of an eighth car in February 1938. The coach bodies were teak-framed on all-welded steel underframes and with exterior steel panels covered with 'Rexine', an ICI coated cloth product in silver grey, no thicker than the interior panels.

The coach underframes were faired to within ten inches of the rail, the bogies being increased from 8ft 6in to 10ft 0in after running experience had been gained. Gresley was always anxious to improve braking performance and after Quick Service Valves were tried successfully on the West Riding Limited when new in 1937, these

Interior of the First class dining car of the Silver Jubilee on its first revenue-earning arrival from Newcastle at King's Cross. While obviously comfortable, the furnishing and decor can hardly be described as 'streamlined'. This is a press picture, the 'passenger' being the photographer's colleague, a Tyneside journalist preparing his 'copy' for telephoning back to the North East.
(*National Railway Museum*)

were fitted ultimately to all streamlined sets before the war intervened, along with automatic slack adjusters to improve riding. Indiarubber sheeting covered the space between coach-ends, much in the way suggested by Bel Geddes in his book *Horizons* in 1932. Interestingly, an earlier author, Chapman Dendy Marshall, had in 1925 suggested storing waterproofed canvases in vertical spring-roller casings, to be extended across the inter-coach gaps on every passenger train as a matter of course.

The livery was 'the most aesthetically pleasing of any train', opines Michael Harris in his history of Gresley's coaching-stock. To round off the silver-grey livery, stainless steel trim and Gill Sans lettering and numbering were applied, while the roofs were spray painted in an aluminium shade over a white lead base. Lettering four inches high reading 'THE SILVER JUBILEE' featured in silver on a dark-blue background to identify the train, if such identity was still thought necessary, while the underframe fairings and bogie frames were painted lead-grey, the wheels and axleboxes being black.

From south to north, the train when new consisted of an Open Brake and Semi-open First articulated as a twin (with only three bogies in place of the usual four), followed by a triplet set consisting of a First Restaurant car, Kitchen car, and Third Restaurant car. Second from front was a Third class, with a Brake Third behind the tender, the two making up a twin. From February 1938, to meet demand, an additional coach was inserted between the northernmost two, unusually taking the Brake's running number, and this twin became a triplet. This would make (from 1938) an eight-coach train running on no more than eleven bogies.

Internally, 'Rexine' in a variety of colours featured prominently in the panelling, while the upholstery sported 'jazz' patterns. Metal fittings were chrome-plated, and the First class compartments were illuminated by vertical Art Deco type candle striplights, in addition to ceiling lighting. The First restaurant car was panelled in Australian maple with blue upholstery, and boasted a Wilton carpet on sponge rubber underlay. The Third restaurant car was panelled in quartered teak with seating in green. Electric heating was used in the kitchen, the car being equipped with two 10kw generators. The overall effect internally, as can be seen from the accompanying illustration, was one of comfort rather than style.

Pressure ventilation was used throughout the train, the sealed windows being double with a quarter-inch space between the glass. Spaces within the coach frames were packed with insulating material to reduce noise, effecting a reduction from 65 to 60 decibels compared to a conventionally constructed train travelling at 70mph in open country – not perhaps a major improvement.

When run as an eight-car set, the Silver Jubilee accommodated 233 seated passengers in its 248 ton tare weight, only 11 fewer than a conventional passenger rake of the time would have done, at the cost of an extra twenty tons tare weight. In its first two years, the set was to notch up 277,370 miles, 162,030 (58 per cent) at 75mph.

* * *

Histories of Britain's railways between the wars record Friday 27 September 1935 as nothing less than a sensational landmark in express train running, when the new A4 Pacific No 2509 *Silver Link* pulled out of platform 6 at King's Cross with its seven-coach rake of silver coaches. And historic it certainly was, although there had already been hints of what was to come. A technical periodical published on that very date, and carrying news from anything up to ten days earlier, reported that 'preliminary trials' had already been carried out with the new locomotive and train, the 29 miles of the Peterborough–Grantham section of the East Coast main line being traversed (uphill) in 26 minutes start-to-stop and six miles covered downhill in the opposite direction at an average of 100mph. No further details of this trial (either on 20 or 22 September) are recorded in the official histories, although it goes some way to explain the impressive confidence with which the LNER's management and staff approached the 27 September trial for an invited but technically discerning complement.

Before they set off, Britain's first streamlined rail travellers were treated to lunch by the LNER, with Ralph Wedgwood, chief general manager, making a speech in which he emphasised that no records were going to be attempted on the forthcoming run – historians can only guess whether he was being cautious or misleading – as, in his words, 'this is not a stunt train'. His was a professional attitude, deliberately not putting pressure on the train crew to break records, and he generously paid tribute to the GWR for pioneering high-speed services in Britain. Coal was being given a chance to show what it could do in reply to newer types of power, he argued.

The travellers who sampled this innovatory train – all of them male, it was noticed at the time – included Cecil J. Allen, actually a company employee, but not likely to be accused by anyone of partisanship in describing the resulting return trip to Grantham with the words 'To such a premiere, British locomotive history finds no parallel whatsoever'. Four world records were set up by No 2509 *Silver Link* – including the world's fastest *verified* speed for a steam locomotive (112mph), and probably the highest ever achieved on the former Great Northern main line at any location other than Stoke Bank (at Arlesey). Other records included the running of 43 miles at not less than 100mph.

C. J. Allen occupied a compartment in the leading Brake Third where he hoped to be undisturbed with his stopwatches and notepads. This was not to be; not only was he joined by Randolph Churchill reporting for the *Daily Mail*, but Gresley himself took a seat in the compartment, followed by Charles Brown, the line's chief civil engineer. Apparently the latter became increasingly uncomfortable as the journey progressed. Speed rose into triple figures – but some of the curves and crossovers provided increasingly rough riding. At the south end of Hatfield a bad shock was experienced, but Gresley, completely imperturbable, directed what Allen described as 'shafts of wit' at the unfortunate Brown, on the subject of his permanent way. The latter was becoming more and more apprehensive as Hitchin flashed past at 107mph and the next 27 miles to Huntingdon were accomplished in just over 15 minutes. Meanwhile, the Offord curves had drawn nigh, in acknowledgement of which driver Taylor slowed to 85mph – on curves which were later to carry a 70mph restriction.

Former King's Cross railwayman-turned-author, P. N. Townend, has immortalised an exchange which took place on the swaying footplate of *Silver Link* between the driver and its designer on that coruscating September afternoon in 1935. Apparently, Gresley had come through the corridor tender to tick off Driver Taylor for going too fast, saying 'Ease your arm young man, we have touched 112mph twice'. This seems to have astonished Taylor who pointed out that the Flaman speed recorder was not operating properly and that he estimated that the highest speed was around 90mph. Townend quite reasonably believes that such a new and vital piece of equipment was unlikely to be inaccurate, but in later years he noticed a tendency for the speed needle to stick against the second needle, a setting indicator – which had been set at 90mph on this occasion. The speed needle could be loosened by knocking on the glass of the recorder. In other words the records of 27 September 1935 may have been made by accident! Gresley's final admonition to Taylor was 'Go a bit easier, we have an old director in the back; he is getting a bit touchy.'!

Driver Taylor later recalled that one of the two inspectors on the down trip felt that boiler pressure was

The down Silver Jubilee approaches Wood Green on a Friday evening, 19 June 1936 with No 2512 *Silver Fox* in the charge of Driver Peachey. His philosophy towards driving a streamlined train was 'take it easy and don't worry!' (*Millbrook House*)

too low on the climb from King's Cross and had ordered the fireman to redouble his efforts. His work certainly could not be faulted thereafter! As to the question of the speed, Taylor later recalled 'Quite frankly I didn't think we'd been going much above 90mph and apparently it was smoother on the engine than in the train'.

The LNER senior staff should really have looked more carefully at this whole question of speed indication. It was quite obvious that their footplate staff were not sufficiently briefed on speed reading; indeed, the fact that their speedometers *recorded* speeds and that insufficiently safe observance of speed restrictions was punishable, created a punitive atmosphere for the crews to work in. Travel fast, yes, but overdo it by even a few mph, and disciplinary action would result.

Despite this, the newspaper reception to *Silver Link's* achievement must have warmed the hearts of LNER managers and staff. One syndicated reporter told the nation's readers of the train 'shooting and winding through the countryside like a silver snake', and there was more, in great and complimentary detail. *Silver Link* was described imaginatively as 'charging with its head down', surely the most anthropomorphic description the daily press has ever published about a steam engine. Even newspaper readers far from London, Darlington, or Newcastle, were able to savour the words of Driver Taylor ('not particularly sooty after the double journey') who described the new Pacific thus:

'The finest engine we have ever had. There is no vibration whatever . . . we could easily have gone faster if we had wanted to – we were not all out by any means.'

Taylor's comments may well show his ignorance of just how fast his train was travelling – as already observed, LNER drivers were not exactly encouraged to attain high speeds regularly in everyday service – and he may well have thought he was doing around 70mph at the Offord curves. Allen believed that the riding of the train was really not acceptable initially, and that there was insufficient compression allowed for in the springs controlling lateral

Gresley's A4 Pacific proved so successful that members of the class were employed on general express duties up and down the East Coast line, in addition to lightweight streamline trains. Here the doyen of the class, No 2509 *Silver Link*, is seen on a more utilitarian train than the one the locomotive was designed to haul. (*RAS Marketing*)

movements. At the same time, relations between the mechanical, operating, and civil engineering departments were not as good as they should have been, he argued in his book *British Pacific Locomotives*, while the technology of 'canting' (or super-elevating) rails at bends was not sufficiently advanced at the time. As final proof of his argument, he cites the habit of the stewards on the Silver Jubilee removing vases of flowers from the dining tables immediately the train started!

Turning from more technical subjects to the matter of comestibles, it is interesting to glimpse what was on the menu on those flowerless tables. The LNER could feel proud in the more than adequate tariff it offered Silver Jubilee travellers, whether they be First class or Third. While awaiting their meal they could enjoy liquid refreshment from a choice of no fewer than 46 cocktails, ranging from 'Adonis' at 1s 3d (7½p) to the 'Silver Jubilee' at 2s 0d (10p). The à la carte menu offered a range of soups from 'real turtle' at 2s 0d or oxtail at 6d (2½p), followed by a fish course (Dover sole at our equivalent of 12½p or oysters at 15p for a half-dozen), before tackling a Jubilee mixed grill – consisting of cutlet, kidney, sausage, tomato and mushrooms, all for 12½p – rounded off by a peach melba at 1s 0d (5p), or cheese and biscuits at half that price. Even vegetarians were catered for, being offered a special risotto at 8d (3½p).

All this was very impressive when compared to the cold buffet offered travellers on the German railcars before 1936, although it should be remembered that in Germany there has always been a tradition of cold food catering, particularly varied sausage-meats, which, with a selection of cheeses and breadstuffs washed down by wine, would not make any German pause to think the fare offered him inadequate. Nevertheless, Gresley and his team had to consider the more demanding culinary requirements of British businessmen and met this catering challenge fully.

Literary appetites were catered for by a W. H. Smith initiative whereby passengers were able to hire brand-new books for their journey. It seems a curious idea for a firm presumably interested in selling books to the public, and the *Railway Gazette*, obviously well aware of publishing developments in Britain at the time, pointed out the idiosyncrasy of such a scheme at a time when paperback editions of quality literature were becoming available for sixpence (2½p) each.

*   *   *

'London has now become a suburb of Newcastle' a first day traveller on the Jubilee told the *Newcastle Journal*. The LNER invited the municipal heads of Newcastle and Darlington to visit this new suburb on the first up train, and considerable publicity was thereby generated by the northern press. Perhaps it was not really necessary – the whole north-east of England seemed to be aware of the introduction of this 'silver arrow shining through the silver grey of a wet September morning' (the *Journal* again), judging by the packed station platforms and strings of spectators by the railside. On the return journey, for example, Darlington was reported as being 'black with people', standing ten deep in places!

Nor did this euphoria dissipate overnight. Writing later in the autumn of 1935, the *Railway Gazette* reckoned that the new train would 'qualify to rank with the established sights of the capital', and went on to elaborate in a manner that confirmed the publicity value of the Silver Jubilee:

'All the ingredients of spectacle are there, from the military smartness of the train attendants to the growing tension as half past five approaches . . . this little nightly pageant must surely react to the benefit of the railways as a whole.'

While this seems all very *Boys' Own Book of Trains* type enthusiasm, *any* kind of interest or excitement that could be generated by a train was ultimately to the railway company's benefit. The crowds which watched the train's departure at King's Cross represented potential future custom, while at Darlington the daily issue of platform tickets nearly trebled when the Jubilee started running. These were encouraging portents of a railway hitting back at its competitors by *creating* a market. Who knows, had the LNER and its sister companies not troubled to do so by introducing intentionally 'flash' services, might there have been much greater public demand for a motorway system earlier than there was, and a much-reduced market for today's InterCity trains?

*   *   *

Tyneside's new link with the Thames left Newcastle (Central) at 10.00am each weekday and Darlington at 10.42am, arriving at King's Cross at 2.00pm. The return journey began at 5.30pm, arriving at Darlington at 8.48pm and Newcastle at 9.30pm. The advertised average speed was 67.08mph, it being obvious that the section north of

Darlington was not mile-a-minute. South of Darlington, therefore, the 232 miles had to be covered in 198 minutes in each direction, an average of 70.3mph.

In its first week, the Silver Jubilee made ten journeys, of which nine were early or punctual. Ironically, on the first down trip, Newcastle was reported by the technical press as having been reached between two and three minutes late, apparently because of a slow recovery from a signal check on the North Eastern section. This was probably inevitable since a 70mph limit had been slapped on the train's progress north of York following sudden doubts about its ability to stop quickly in the colour-light sections. Interestingly, the *Newcastle Journal*, while reporting that the first down arrival appeared to be two minutes late, was told officially that the train was punctual 'by King's Cross time', a phrase it published without explanation. Presumably, this simply meant that the Central clock was wrong, and that the train had arrived four hours after

The second A4, No 2510 *Quicksilver*, picks up water at Langley troughs, the last set of troughs before London, on the up Silver Jubilee, around 1936, when the locomotive still sported its name painted in the middle of the streamline casing. *(RAS Marketing)*

leaving London, but the lateness does appear to have entered the record books.

The second week produced one late arrival in London by some five minutes, following a points failure en route, but there were also two early arrivals on this fastest of schedules – one each of five and four minutes respectively. All this despite the reportedly 'very bad' weather experienced in that first fortnight.

Two up journeys recorded on 30 September and 2 October respectively – the first and third ever made – reached King's Cross within 45 seconds of each other, and both early into the bargain. Interestingly, the two runs were never more than 67 seconds apart at any timing-point, indicating the precision employed in both timetabling and operation. However, both trains ran behind time as far south as Grantham, confirming that the northern section of the run was not as suited to high speed as the former GNR main line. Indeed, some authors such as Cecil J. Allen had over the years frequently written critically of express running on the former North Eastern section of the East Coast main line. To be fair, it is perfectly possible that the comparative lack of water troughs north of Doncaster – there was only one set (at Wiske Moor) in a 122-mile stretch from Scrooby to

Newcastle – may have had a psychological effect in inhibiting crews from running as fast as they would further south, where there were four sets of troughs in 146 miles. The task was not made any easier for the A4s' crews by the imposition of the 70mph limit, particularly since the up Darlington–York schedule, start-to-pass, required the illegal average speed of 70mph! Even though the overall Newcastle–York timing start-to-pass was little more than 60mph, including the Darlington stop, this could hardly be maintained without having to go over seventy at some stage of the 80-mile stretch.

* * *

Below is a summary of these first and third southbound runs, the first timed by Brian Reid, the second by Cecil J. Allen and R. E. Charlewood:

	Schedule from Darlington Minutes	Actual	
		30/9/35	2/10/35
York, pass	37	40.41	39.57
Doncaster, pass	67	69.38	69.47
Grantham, pass	110	109.18	110.17
Peterborough, pass	134	131.57	132.07
Hitchin, pass	171	167.27	166.47
King's Cross, arrive	198	195.51	195.08

This is precision time-keeping, testimony to a high calibre performance from both crew and machine. (Note the evidence in the second column of a 21 minute 50 second run at an average of 81.5mph over the 29.7 miles between Grantham and Peterborough, Stoke Summit included.) Yet the LNER had put virtually no effort whatsoever into training its locomotive men for high-speed running, something that as has already been remarked they were hardly called upon to do very much of in previous years. Nor was there much opportunity for the men to get to know the new locomotive well before embarking on the service, with only three weeks available for such a familiarisation process.

Notice too, the use of the singular noun 'locomotive'. *Silver Link* operated the train in solitary splendour for nearly three weeks, the second A4, No 2510 *Quicksilver*, not being rostered to the service until 17 October. Shed allocation records show that the pioneer was allocated to King's Cross but was shedded overnight at Gateshead, and it was there one night during the train's first two weeks of operation that an intrepid Tyneside fitter carried out urgent repairs to *Silver Link*'s brick arch *inside*

the firebox. Gresley was reportedly shocked at what this must have involved. The modern reader can only despair at the working conditions that railwaymen were expected to accept – or were prepared to volunteer for – in order to preserve the company's image of operating a silver locomotive on a silver train under the eye of the nation's press.

Emergencies apart, the London depot of King's Cross operated the service in both directions, two crews being responsible. The first would travel down to Newcastle on the Sunday on the 12.40pm ex-King's Cross, returning with the up Jubilee on the following day and on the Wednesday and Friday, going down again with the Jubilee on Tuesday and Thursday. The second pair of footplatemen worked the down service on Monday, Wednesday and Friday, and the up service on Tuesday and Thursday, returning to London on the Saturday with the 'Junior Scotsman' in summer or the Flying Scotsman during the rest of the year when it stopped at Newcastle.

By the summer of 1938 it had become unusual for the locomotive off the up service to return to Newcastle that evening, and indeed was often seen working the down West Riding Limited. Nevertheless, allocation records show that, of the first four A4s, only No 2511 was based at Gateshead. No 2510, another King's Cross engine, was kept in reserve at the southern end to cover possible failure on the down service. Not until the third locomotive, No 2511 *Silver King*, was available could the up Jubilee expect a streamlined substitute engine. Needless to say, when the train experienced its first locomotive failure early in its career, it happened at the northern end!

It was symptomatic of the LNER's apparently threadbare approach to the introduction of its streamlined express services that, for the six weeks after the train began running, there was no proper relief locomotive available at the northern end. On 4 November, *Silver Link* was unable to take up the roster and A3 No 2503 *Firdaussi* substituted. No details appear to have been recorded of the resulting run, although it is pleasant to record that the unstreamlined Pacific was into King's Cross with a minute to spare – 239 minutes as against sister engine *Papyrus*'s 232, but with a stop at Darlington included. (Interestingly, *Firdaussi* was very much Gateshead's 'form horse' in 1935; eight months before this, the locomotive had brought the Flying Scotsman up to London in 233 minutes from Darlington, including 6½ minutes spent in station stops, this with 445 tons.)

Once the third A4 was available, it stood pilot at

Gateshead each weekday until the Jubilee was adjudged safely on its way, and then operated a mid-morning Leeds–Glasgow service from Newcastle to Edinburgh and back, thus covering 250 revenue-earning miles daily – a highly economical use of a standby engine. (One retrospective source suggests that the standby roster was even more productive, the A4 taking the up Glasgow–Leeds train on to York before returning to Tyneside to take up its post, thus adding an additional 160 miles to the diagram.) When all four silver A4s were available – the last was No 2512 *Silver Fox* – three were based at King's Cross, one of their regular rosters comprising the 7.30pm down Aberdonian to Grantham returning with an up meat and fish fitted freight arriving at Finsbury Park at 2.12 the next morning. There could scarcely be a better demonstration of the versatility of the class, or indeed of the concept of using steam locomotives for the new service, as opposed to diesel railcars.

However, the 4 November breakdown illustrated that there had been hardly any time for 'teething troubles' to be ironed out in either locomotive or coaching stock before the 30 September inauguration; yet again, one can only marvel at the company's enormous confidence in Nigel Gresley's ability to design and put into traffic a train of unprecedented appearance and function without extensive trials.

The only mechanical breakdown en route in the train's first year occurred on 4 September 1936 when No 2510 had to come off the up service at York. Unfortunately the standby engine, a C7/2 Atlantic No 732 (a former NER Class Z), was unfamiliar to Driver Samwells of King's Cross and he made a special stop at Doncaster to exchange this Atlantic for another, more 'user friendly', as it were. His new mount was C1 No 4452, a former Great Northern engine, and with it he and his fireman ran the 156 miles to London in the excellent time of 139 minutes. This represented an average speed of 67.3mph and meant that the older engine had actually *dropped* time, although it should be remembered that this section of the journey would normally be a pass-to-stop timing (131 minutes), and not start-to-stop.

Another failure on the Jubilee under way (there were apparently only ten out of 1,952 journeys) is recorded in the reminiscences of King's Cross driver Charlie Peachey. On 17 August 1937, while driving No 2510, he detected a smoking tender axlebox on a down run between Grantham and Newark, and stopped at the first signalbox. Arranging to requisition the locomotive of a stopping

train at Newark, he and his mate soon found themselves on the footplate of an Atlantic with a loose tender connection tipping coal on them from the back of the tender. They replaced this with A3 No 2596 *Manna* at Doncaster, and Newcastle was reached 25 minutes late, with a few minutes regained north of York.

Peachey believed that the Jubilee was much easier to run than the Coronation, and evidently found the duty fairly lucrative. The balancing Saturday working involved taking the Scarborough Flyer down to York and back for what he described as 'two days' pay for 11 hours work'. His attitude to working the fastest trains on the system, incidentally, was delightfully carefree – 'there was no strain in driving a streamliner, all you had to do was to take it easy and not worry'!

On Thursday 27 August 1936, the LNER conducted a remarkable double dynamometer-car trial on the Silver Jubilee on both up and down journeys. The newest of the A4s, No 2512 *Silver Fox* was selected for the southbound journey, with the load increased to 270 tons. Writing in post war years, Geoffrey Freeman Allen recalled that he had gone specially to King's Cross to see the Jubilee arrive that day because he knew that an attempt was to be made down Stoke Bank to beat the 112mph attained by *Silver Link*. If this was so, then it was unfortunate that the information made available to London's railway enthusiasts was not also passed to Driver George Haygreen on *Silver Fox*! It appears that the engine had to be pushed hard to reach a new maximum of 113mph, and in so doing, the middle big-end had come close to disintegration; indeed, the dynamometer car underframe was hit by debris from the cylinder dropping to the ballast, and London was reached seven minutes late 'with steam spurting angrily from between the frames', as Allen recalled. The technical press did not get wind of this pyrrhic victory, the *Railway Gazette* reporting that lunch was being served without any problems in the train itself as the record speed was reached.

It was a different matter on the footplate. Seemingly the unfortunate driver was simply not briefed about the plan to go for a maximum speed, and the A4 really had not attained a high enough climbing speed on the northern scarp of Stoke summit or high enough boiler pressure before launching itself and its train down the famous slope towards the record books. Haygreen later recalled:

'No inspector came on the footplate and we got

instructions by the telephone from the (dynamometer) car – but the inspector in the car had said "We won't interfere with you" . . . after going gently through Grantham we were asked by telephone message at Corby to top 100, going all out.'

Despite the misunderstanding, the LNER had set up what is believed to be the British record speed for a steam-powered train carrying fare-paying passengers; the speed of 113mph was never equalled in revenue-earning service during the age of steam, only Bill Hoole coming close to it in 1959 with his A4 No 60007 *Sir Nigel Gresley*, and a train-load of enthusiasts itching for a new world record. Poor Driver Haygreen in 1936; he was certainly the victim of ineffective communication by management.

The northbound journey which followed was unspectacular but successful, something of a swansong for veteran driver Bill Sparshatt, and he relished the run so much that he insisted that a full glass of water be placed on the dynamometer car floor to record any imperfections in riding junctions or points. In fact, while nothing spilled at these parts of the run, a slight spill did occur on a malefactory straight. Meanwhile, the locomotive, *Silver Link* once again, went over Stoke summit at 75mph with this increased load, promptly blowing-off steam in a 23 minute 9 second transit of the Peterborough–Grantham section. Darlington was reached 3¼ minutes early with 130 miles being completed at an average of 80mph.

After its first twelve months of operation, the LNER was able to report that its premier train had completed two journeys short of 500, of which 278 arrivals were early. In the whole of July 1936 *every* arrival at King's Cross was at least one minute early, an astonishing record for a working whose schedule was unprecedentedly demanding. Altogether 133,464 miles had been covered, all but one return journey being made by the stock specially built for it, with 115,536 miles being run at an average of 70mph, and 30,000 miles at 80mph.

Punctuality over the first two years was reported by Mr Townend as being 72 per cent in the down direction and 68 per cent in the up, although it is not clear if this included early arrivals. If this were so, this was a surprisingly disappointing record, since the Coronation, covering an additional 124.5 miles and conveying either eight or nine vehicles, never achieved less than 77 per cent punctual and early arrivals in either direction in any sample this author has examined. Possibly the Jubilee's performance

was delayed by other traffic movements which did not affect the later streamliner, which, for example, neither entered nor left London during a peak travelling period. On the other hand, the down Jubilee, which left during the evening rush hour, performed better than the up train. A report credited the up service with only one late arrival in London between 27 October and 25 November 1938, and only then because of dense fog.

In August 1938 that doyen of railway recorders, Cecil J. Allen, published two logs of down journeys he had recently made on the train. In the first, No 4467 *Wild Swan* started so quickly from King's Cross that it was soon signal-checked and was running 90 seconds late at Hatfield. This seemed to act as another spur to high-speed progress and 100mph was achieved at Conington, and the Peterborough–Grantham section was completed in 22 minutes 46 seconds, including an average of 82.3mph for the 15.3 miles up Stoke Bank and 76.5mph over the top. Even after subsequent easy running, Darlington was reached three minutes early.

On CJA's second journey, No 2512 *Silver Fox* was 4½ minutes late at Huntingdon, but then ran with such effect as to make up 8¼ minutes by Northallerton. Nearly 80mph was averaged up Stoke and no less than 94mph achieved on the level north of York. With 15 miles run at an average of 90.6mph on this stretch – the 70mph limit was now abandoned – Darlington was reached in the best ever time, in Mr Allen's experience, of 194 minutes 39 seconds, 3½ minutes early.

As late as one year after the introduction of the Jubilee, on 28 September 1936, Wedgwood issued a memo recommending that £14,768 be spent on improving the placing, and thus the sighting, of distant semaphore signals. Pointing out that 55 distants on the Great Northern section, 88 on the Great Eastern, and 16 on the Great Central, required to be re-located farther from their respective home signals, or even be themselves preceded by a distant distant, as it were, Wedgwood went on:

'it has been found that trains running at eighty to ninety mph require from 1,200 to 1,800 yards, according to gradient, for adequate braking purposes . . . A number of cases have recently occurred in which experienced drivers have over-run the home signal for a considerable distance although the brake was fully applied before the distant signal was reached and although the rails were sanded.'

Again, this is evidence of the LNER's less than professional approach to the operation of these streamlined expresses. A locomotive whose streamlined outline was designed in a borrowed wind tunnel, crewed by men with little or no experience of high-speed conditions (despite Wedgwood's comment above), running over a network lacking any kind of cab-signalling apparatus, and with (as the chief general manager conceded) inadequate braking distance between many of the signals – despite all this, the Silver Jubilee was a success. One can only marvel at the improvisatory ingenuity of the British railwayman.

*   *   *

Two interesting memories of travelling on the Silver Jubilee come from Michael Joyce and Ray Cox. Michael was a teenage office-boy in Leeds in 1936 and was lucky enough to be sent on a journey to London via Darlington by his employer. It appears that his enlightened boss was so impressed by young Mr Joyce's publication of a railway newsletter within the office that he was sent on an all-expenses-paid trip to get this nonsense out of his system! Michael recalls standing on Darlington platform, among apparently sophisticated passengers, awaiting the streamliner with some trepidation, as can be imagined. He was interested to note that a preceding London express was headed by the Gateshead reserve engine No 2511, the Jubilee itself being powered by No 2510 *Quicksilver*.

Understandably, the journey southwards 'flashed past as quickly as the train passed through stations'. At King's Cross, a posse of photographers was waiting on the platform, and Michael learned that one of his fellow passengers was Crown Prince Olav of Norway. Unknown to him, the prince had visited the footplate before departure from Newcastle, and had asked the driver for the engine's horsepower rating. Driver Peachey recalled in his own words (recorded later) 'Well, I did not know, I had never thought about it, so I changed the subject and told him the boiler pressure'. Evidence yet again of the LNER's lack of any special training for operating the new generation of high speed trains which were always likely to attract public attention.

Before leaving London, Michael was allowed to visit

A 1939 shot of the Silver Jubilee speeding through New Barnet on its way northwards behind blue-liveried No 2510 *Quicksilver*. *(Millbrook House)*

the locomotive depot opposite the terminus, where *Quicksilver* was being prepared for the return journey. The young enthusiast was allowed to sit in the Pacific's cab as the engine was turned on the turntable, but he was unable to return north on the streamliner – instead, he had to 'slum it' back to Leeds on the Pullman!

Ray Cox not only enjoyed a northbound trip on the Jubilee on 2 August 1939 as a reward for passing exams, but returned south to London the next day on what was one of the fastest journeys the Coronation ever made (of which more later). On his Jubilee trip, he recalls he occupied seat 145, a right-hand corner seat, being moved to First class seat No 46 at Darlington by a friendly steward. *Silver Link* brought the express into Newcastle one minute early.

* * *

Obviously, the need to lengthen the rake from seven to eight vehicles in 1938 was evidence of the success of the Silver Jubilee. In its first week of operation, beginning on 30 September 1935, the train carried an average of 130 passengers up and 149 down, but by the second week the average complement was 146 up and 171 down. Since these are average figures for the five days of operation in each week, it is obvious that there must have been occasions when every seat was taken, the technical press at the time commenting that it was already proving necessary to seat passengers in the restaurant cars from the start of the journey.

The train's loadings throughout its first year, however, worked out at 136 passengers per train; a surprisingly low figure, given the early loadings. (68,000 passengers were carried, announced the railway press in the autumn of 1936, in 498 journeys.) Nevertheless, on 21 April 1936 the Institute of Transport was told by Robert Bell, the LNER's assistant general manager, that the Jubilee was earning 16s 2d (81p) per mile (including restaurant car takings) against working expenses (general charges,

interest, and depreciation) of 4s 2d (21p). Bell argued that the net income of 12s (60p) was more than twice the net earning per mile of the average LNER passenger service.

A slightly different set of figures was made available to the LNER board some 18 months later, and these are listed, in comparison with the company's later stream-lined trains' earnings, on page 120. The difference between the two sets of figures of five pence per mile is probably explained by Bell's calculations being made on the basis of a seven-coach train, which had swelled to eight by July 1938. Obviously, the Jubilee enjoyed a satisfactory surplus of revenue over costs, although not as much as the 700 per cent claimed by one historian. He discovered that the London–Tyneside traffic had increased by 12.4 per cent in the ten months since the Jubilee's introduction, although it has to be pointed out that it had increased by 6.2 per cent in the ten months previously, with no extra outlay.

Nevertheless, there was no doubting the financial success of the enterprise, particularly with Gresley's comment about the train's 'first cost' being paid for by supplementary fares alone within three years. He made this pronouncement in a Presidential address to the Institution of Mechanical Engineers not long after being knighted in 1936. Describing the implementary cost of the first locomotive and coaches as £34,500 (interestingly, half that of the reported cost of the first US Zephyr, but carrying twice the passenger complement of the diesel), Gresley reported that £12,000 had been collected in supplementary fares alone in one year's working. This commercial success was matched by the train's operation. Only ten failures en route in 1,952 journeys was highly commendable, particularly since a new class of locomotive was involved. This failure rate of 0.5 per cent compared favourably with the Coronation's 3.5 per cent, and over a longer period.

Britain's first streamlined train service came to an end, like the other streamliners, on Thursday 31 August 1939. The last arrival in London was behind No 4489 *Dominion*

of Canada, with the final working of all taken to Newcastle by No 4499 *Sir Murrough Wilson*. It was a pity that none of the four silver A4s, all of them by then repainted blue, was available in that final week, although the Operating department obviously had more pressing problems to consider.

* * *

At the LNER's annual general meeting in March 1936, the first since the introduction of the Silver Jubilee, chairman William Whitelaw gave a strangely understated impromptu report on Britain's first streamlined express train.

> 'We required a new train between Newcastle and London because the traffic was too heavy for our existing service. We did not require another *whole* train of the same length as the old trains, and we took this opportunity to put on a train of *moderate* length, which could be run at high speed.'

The *italics* are this author's; the somewhat negative attitude to the Silver Jubilee was entirely Whitelaw's. He had already publicly said that a high-speed service could not be operated on the LNER system; when proved wrong, he publicly dismissed one of Britain's finest transport utilities as half a train! The LNER's 'over capacity' policy towards passenger trains will be discussed in more detail in the Postscript, but Whitelaw's off-the-cuff remarks were evidence indeed of the company's fixation with running gargantuan 15- or 16-coach trains, each vehicle usually occupied well below capacity. Obviously, the Jubilee turned this policy on its head by imposing a limited capacity with supplementary tickets to ensure that such capacity was not exceeded. If Whitelaw thought a seven-coach train was 'moderate', he must have seen the *Fliegende Hamburger* as a ganger's trolley!

5 HASTENING SLOWLY:
THE LMS CORONATION SCOT

The London Midland & Scottish Railway was slow to join the Streamline Age, its Coronation Scot express only emerging some 22 months after the LNER's Silver Jubilee. Indeed, the latter company was introducing the first of its second generation streamliners, the Coronation, on the same day, and on a considerably faster schedule than the LMS newcomer. Not only that, but the rolling-stock for the Coronation Scot came perilously close to being considered a 'patch-up' compared to the specially-built LNER coaches, and the LMS streamlined locomotives, although impressive in outline, were far from being so when examined close up. It was all very disappointing for a company which showed such early awareness of the need to consider streamlining its trains and was prepared to invest in the necessary research.

As we have seen, the LMS commissioned research at the National Physical Laboratory on overcoming air resistance to trains as early as 1931, around the same time that the Brill railcar was introducing the concept of streamlining to the rail passenger in the USA. Illustrations appearing later in the academic periodical press (specifically, the *Proceedings* of the Institution of Mechanical Engineers, volume 134, 1936) show that a model of a Royal Scot 4–6–0 was the object of air resistance research and was wind-tunnel tested in three different modes – garbed from chimney to rail in an overall casing with vertical frontal wedge; with a domed extension to the smokebox only; and as a control with no embellishments at all. The results were not published until late 1936, by which time the company had a new chief mechanical engineer, W. A. Stanier, and had already seen the LNER pioneer its own services – and not with a vertical-wedge locomotive.

The results of the above tests were publicly endorsed by Sir Nigel Gresley at a meeting of the Mechanical Engineers, but it is a pity that Stanier was not present to comment on whether they were the basis for his, or his

employers', plans for streamlined trains. Stanier was in India at the time, but there is considerable speculation about just how this former Swindon protégé viewed the importance of streamlining.

The late Brian Haresnape has commented that the casings of the Princess Coronation class were 'adopted more to please the (LMS) directors than through any scientific aim'. Certainly, it is difficult to see how the 1931 NPL research could have been the basis for any such streamlining configuration, since neither of the semi-streamlined, or fully-streamlined modes were adopted after testing at Teddington. Nor did the eventual vertically-rounded nose for Stanier's Pacifics feature in the tests, which appear to have been repeated in more detail at the company's own, later, wind tunnel at Derby.

The wind tunnel which decided the shape of the Princess Coronation class of Pacifics was situated at Derby and is here seen in a specially-posed publicity shot in October 1937. The only such research facility owned by a British railway, the tunnel was taken over by the local technical college in 1980. (*National Railway Museum*)

This latter location was where the LMS streamlined Pacifics were conceived, their outward appearance being finalised in the company's scientific research laboratory, unique among the four grouped railways. Set up by the former NPL scientist, F. C. Johansen, and opened on 10 December 1935 by the famous New Zealand-born physicist Lord Rutherford (1871–1937), the laboratory included the company's own wind tunnel. In comparison to the NPL tunnel, which was 60ft long by 7ft square, this was smaller, a rectangular shape 4½ft by 3½ ft. Its length was not specified in the souvenir brochure issued to first-day guests. The motor-driven propeller developed speeds of up to 100ft/second. A 1948 review of the depart-

The fastest journey time between London and Glasgow was achieved, not by one of the streamlined Princess Coronation Pacifics, but by the unstreamlined No 6201 *Princess Elizabeth* in 1936, at an average speed of 70mph, proving that a six-hour schedule was practical. In the event, an extra 30 minutes was allowed the Coronation Scot. The halcyon days of No 46201 were long behind her when she was photographed at Kilmarnock on Sunday 15 April 1962 on a Carlisle–Glasgow parcels train. (W. Hamilton)

ment's work described the wind tunnel's function as testing (at speeds of no higher than 60mph) 'small components such as ventilators, filters, and signal lamps, or small models of trains, buildings, and station awning roofs'. Obviously, post-war research interests no longer ran to the simulated high-speed testing of streamlined locomotive front ends, as it presumably did when the test centre first began operating.

In 1933, Stanier's Princess Royal class had introduced the Pacific wheel arrangement to expresses on the West Coast main line, which had never previously seen anything larger than a 4–6–0. Indeed, the line had been flooded in 1924–5 with Midland Compound 4–4–0s

newly constructed at a time when the rival LNER was building new A1 Pacifics, and the Great Western, Castle 4–6–0s. To the historian, the LMS locomotive policy over the first four years of the company's life was little short of disastrous, with an under-powered locomotive being adopted as standard, and double-heading being confirmed as commonplace. Even when Sir Henry Fowler was asked to introduce a larger 4–6–0 type into traffic in 1927, the design work seems largely to have originated from external influences. The builders of the Royal Scot class, the North British Locomotive Co in Glasgow, appear to have been given considerable freedom in construction – in contrast to the same firm's commission

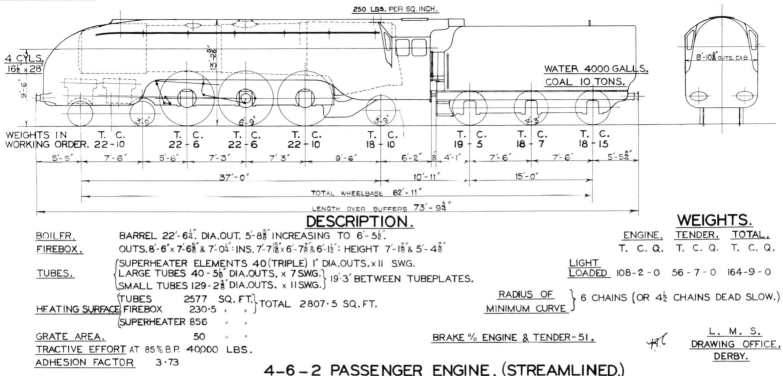

POWER CLASS" 7P.

E.D. Nº 260A

250 LBS. PER SQ. INCH.

4 CYLS. 16½" x 28"

WATER 4000 GALLS. COAL 10 TONS.

8'-10⅝" OUTS. CAB

WEIGHTS IN WORKING ORDER.

T. C.	T. C.	T. C.	T. C.	T. C.	T. C.	T. C.	T. C.	T. C.
22-10	22-6	22-6	22-10	18-10	19-5	18-7	18-15	

5'-5" 7'-6" 5'-6" 7'-3" 7'-3" 9'-6" 6'-2" 4'-1" 7'-6" 7'-6" 5'-5¾"

37'-0"   10'-11"   15'-0"

TOTAL WHEELBASE 62'-11"

LENGTH OVER BUFFERS 73'-9¾"

DESCRIPTION.

BOILER. BARREL 22'-6¼". DIA.OUT. 5'-8⅝" INCREASING TO 6'-5½".

FIREBOX. OUTS.8'-6" x 7'-6⅝" & 7'-0¼": INS. 7'-7⅞" & 6'-7⅞" & 6'-1½": HEIGHT 7'-1⅛" & 5'-4⅞"

TUBES. {SUPERHEATER ELEMENTS 40 (TRIPLE) 1" DIA.OUTS. x 11 S.W.G.
LARGE TUBES 40-5⅛" DIA.OUTS. x 7 S.W.G.}
SMALL TUBES 129-2⅜" DIA.OUTS. x 11 S.W.G.} 19'-3" BETWEEN TUBEPLATES.

HEATING SURFACE. {TUBES 2577 SQ.FT.} TOTAL 2807.5 SQ.FT.
FIREBOX 230.5 " "
SUPERHEATER 856 " "

GRATE AREA. 50 " "

TRACTIVE EFFORT AT 85% B.P. 40,000 LBS.

ADHESION FACTOR 3.73

BRAKE % ENGINE & TENDER = 51.

WEIGHTS.

	ENGINE.			TENDER.			TOTAL.		
	T.	C.	Q.	T.	C.	Q.	T.	C.	Q.
LIGHT LOADED	108	2	0	56	7	0	164	9	0

RADIUS OF MINIMUM CURVE } 6 CHAINS (OR 4½ CHAINS DEAD SLOW.)

L. M. S. DRAWING OFFICE. DERBY.

4–6–2 PASSENGER ENGINE. (STREAMLINED.)

for twenty LNER A1s (later A3s) which were already in service from Gresley's drawing-board.

In other words, the LMS was still finding its way in terms of larger locomotive construction, redoubling the interest engendered by the promised appearance of new streamlined locomotives in 1937. Some observers at the time were so impressed with the Princess Royals that they believed the new locomotives would simply be streamlined versions of Stanier's first Pacifics. After all, one of them had made a resounding impression on the rail community in Britain by accomplishing a double non-stop run between London and Glasgow in November 1936.

On the 16th of that month, No 6201 *Princess Elizabeth* had hauled seven coaches northwards over the 401 miles in slightly less than 354 minutes at an average speed of 68.2mph, Shap and Beattock included. The Princess excelled even this on the next day, returning to London with eight coaches in 344 minutes 20 seconds, at an average of 70mph. It was an outstanding accomplishment

but achieved at some cost. Apparently the locomotive was found to have a defect the day before the outward journey and some frantic preparations had to be undertaken. Any sleep lost could not be made up the next night unfortunately; in Glasgow, the Pacific was found to require a piston re-metalled, so more drastic overnight work was called for. While the engine was equalling the world record for a non-stop steam-hauled train – 401 miles, achieved on successive days – this was only eight miles more than the distance attained five days a week by Gresley's Pacifics on the East Coast with no such air of desperation. Admittedly the average speed was higher; indeed to average 70mph between Glasgow and London was highly commendable, particularly with no means of relieving the crew.

In fact, the Pacifics for the new streamlined service were to be a different class from the Princess Royals, although quite visibly a development of the older engine. One author, J. W. P. Rowledge, contends that as early as March 1935 a ¹⁄₂₄-scale model of a streamlined Princess

Official drawing of Stanier's Princess Coronation Pacific. *(National Railway Museum)*

Royal was prepared in a vertical-style casing, complete with the footplate projecting slightly round the front of the engine, very much like the Borsig 4–6–4 in Germany.

When the first LMS streamlined engines were ordered they were to be numbered 6213–7 as a continuation of the Princess Royals, before Stanier made a number of changes which effectively created a new class of Pacifics. Apart from the streamlined casing, these had larger driving wheels (6ft 9in compared with 6ft 6in) and a larger firebox, which almost filled the loading gauge. Like their 1933 predecessors they had four cylinders and 250 lb/sq in boiler pressure. One historian of LMS locomotives credits T. F. Coleman with having undertaken much of the detailed design work, which was virtually rubber-stamped by Stanier. The new locomotives were officially given the name Princess Coronation class in September 1937.

The 'baby whale' of British railway streamlining. That American opinion of the LMS Pacific comes to mind when viewing the Princess Coronation's front-end. Note the handles which allowed the front to open into a 'bat's wing' configuration to allow access to the smokebox. In this 1938 shot, No 6221 *Queen Elizabeth* is standing at Rugby on a non-streamlined express. *(Millbrook House)*

The streamlining was vertical in alignment compared with the A4, although in fact the front sloped quite considerably. From a frontal view, for example, it would not be obvious that the centre of the chimney orifice was no less than 10ft from the front buffer edges. The casing was cut away over the driving wheels, giving an impression of power, very much like Dreyfuss's design for the Mercury class K5 Pacifics on the New York Central. This was confirmed by American transport author Robert Reed, who believed the new LMS locomotive looked 'more American' than Gresley's streamlined Pacific. He went farther, commenting 'the locomotive was as smooth and plain as a baby whale . . . though quite blind on the front and in need of some anthropomorphic eyes'.

More practically, both J. F. Clay and O. S. Nock have insisted that the LMS streamlining was superior to that of the LNER A4, offering less air resistance at speeds above 75mph, although Clay conceded that the driver's view could be obscured by drifting exhaust when the engine was working less than flat out. When unstreamlined, all engines in the class eventually were to be fitted with massive smoke deflectors, whether they were originally streamlined or not. One unattractive aspect of the streamlining, to this author at least, was the prominent riveting visible on the upper surfaces, giving the casing a temporary appearance (quite appropriately, as it happened), and in contrast to the A4's casing which was an integral part of the locomotive's design.

The tender carried only 4,000 gallons of water, but this was thought sufficient on a line where there were no fewer than eleven water-troughs. As was seen with the tender originally supplied for the A4s, where a ton of coal was sacrificed for a more streamlined shape, this was a potentially limiting parameter for the class when it entered more general service, and indeed may have been one of the reasons why these Pacifics were not to be as

A streamlined Princess Coronation Pacific under construction at Crewe. The tapering smokebox and ribbed supports for the casing are very noticeable, as is one of the hinged streamline doors lying in the foreground. *(National Railway Museum)*

War was not long in the future when this summer 1939 picture was taken at Crewe. No 6238 *City of Carlisle* is nearing completion in the background and would be outshopped in September 1939 – when the rival LNER was putting its streamlined engines into store. (*RAS Marketing*)

long-lived as their streamlined rivals on the East Coast.

Some of the later members of the LMS class, which was still building during and after World War II, saw less than 20 years' service (the streamlined Nos 6246/7, for example), whereas none of the A4s worked for fewer than 24 years (apart from No 4469 *Sir Ralph Wedgwood*, lost to bombing at York on 29 April 1942), and two came close to celebrating their 30th anniversaries in normal service. Yet the LMS Pacific was built, certainly in its unstreamlined form, with ease of maintenance very much in mind, and really should have had longer usefulness. It was the A4, not the Duchess class (as the Princess Coronations were usually known) that was sent for when diesels had to be replaced on the Glasgow–Aberdeen route in 1962 – a line which had been LMS territory. The Duchess tenders' limited water capacity must have had something to do with this; significantly, when one of the class was tested over Southern metals on the Atlantic Coast Express in 1948, an Austerity class 5,000 gallon tender had to be attached in place of the LMS vehicle.

Nevertheless, no less than ten tons of coal were carried – a record for a British tender – and there was

A front-end profile of either No 6223 or 6224 at Crewe on an unknown pre-war date. Apart from illustrating casing detail, this side view shows the 'Mercury' wings on the locomotive's buffer-beam headlamps; a fascinating 'streamlined' detail. (*Millbrook House*)

LMS streamlined Pacifics on parade in 1937. From left to right, Nos 6222 *Queen Mary*, 6221 *Queen Elizabeth*, and 6220 *Coronation*, pose for the camera at Crewe Works, complete with express headlamps.   (*British Rail*)

room for a coal pusher, a small 10½in steam cylinder which could be activated to ram coal forward towards the fireman. It was an interesting innovation (although believed borrowed from the Borsig 05 4–6–4 in Germany) on a locomotive which was perhaps disappointing in not incorporating more. Why no corridor in the tender, for example? Gresley had never patented the corridor tender in the United Kingdom (although he apparently did in the USA) and its use would have permitted the Carlisle stop to be eliminated and a faster schedule introduced. The company must have been considering this possibility. In 1937 one such vehicle began construction at Crewe, although there is little reference to it in contemporary technical literature, and in 1950 it was adapted for normal usage, coupled to a Black Five 4–6–0. While a corridor through the tender

would obviously have reduced coal and water capacity, this could have been compensated for by supplying the Pacifics with eight-wheeled tenders.

* * *

One seminal point from the NPL tests was the suggestion that 'a surprisingly large proportion of the air resistance of a coach . . . is contributed by the bogies and undercarriage structure'. To the researchers' suggestion that articulated stock be used (as it was already on the Silver Jubilee), there was to be an eventual positive response – as we shall see, there were two separate coaching rakes for the Coronation Scot, the first being non-articulated, while the second was.

Just as the streamline casings for the Princess Coronation class were not above criticism, so the coaching stock for the LMS's new Coronation Scot train was also initially disappointing. Far from building a new set of stock, the company refurbished existing vehicles, prompting Messrs Essery and Jenkinson, historians of LMS coach history, to

speculate that 'the evidence . . . does suggest that permission to build the trains may have been granted only if it could be achieved at low cost'.

For a thorough history of this stock, the reader is recommended to read the very detailed work by the above-named authors (see Bibliography), but an outline description is necessary here.

* * *

There were in fact two quite different generations of stock built for this train, in 1937, and again in 1939. The 1937 generation consisted of 27 vehicles, marshalled in three sets of nine coaches each. Each set was designed to run in the following formation: First Brake, First, First Diner, Kitchen Car, two Third Diners, Kitchen Car, Third Diner, and Third Brake. Remarkable was the fact that the kitchen cars utilised gas for cooking and lighting, something which was apparently based on the company's long experience with such arrangements, coupled with an unhappy experiment with electric cooking in 1933.

Nevertheless, the rival LNER was receiving complaints from the public about gas smells from its kitchen cars several years earlier, and the use of gas in a modern 'flagship' express is frankly surprising.

In all, 21 of the 27 vehicles were converted from existing stock, all of it fairly modern, but inevitably attracting a charge of stinginess, in contrast to the LNER's willingness to build from scratch. Only the Brake Firsts and Corridor Firsts were built from new, two for each set. With the construction cost for the entire stock quoted by Essery and Jenkinson as £27,000, of which half was probably spent on the six new vehicles, it appears that the rest of the stock was costed at as little as £700 per coach.

For this, the LMS created a blue-and-silver livery for stock seating 82 First class and 150 Third class passengers. Much use was made of wood panelling from all parts of the British Empire, and even more remarkably in the case of one of the Third class vestibule cars, from the wooden piles under the recently-dismantled Waterloo Bridge, immersed since 1817! Wilton carpeting was used throughout the passenger cars irrespective of class.

LMS historians argue that the company was so far in advance of the LNER in coach design and decoration *before* the streamlined services were introduced, that no revolutionary remodelling was necessary (although they concede that Gresley treated First class passengers better by offering individual armchairs). This is an interesting point of view, one which is acceptable since the LMS was making no attempt to use coaching interiors intensivel any more than did the LNER. The opportunities misse by both companies – to accommodate more passenge per coach without compromising on comfort standarc – will be discussed in the Postscript.

* * *

The eventual decision to build a new generation c coaching stock for the train, apparently taken within thre months of its introduction, is fairly puzzling, particularly a there was no apparent dissatisfaction recorded as to th operation of the 1937 set. Certainly, it was felt that th LMS should exhibit a train at the New York World's Fa in 1939, and this appears to have been the motivation fc the construction of a new set.

On 20 January 1939 a Coronation Scot train, painte in crimson lake with gold stripes, was loaded at South ampton for the USA. There were eight passenge vehicles, including a First class sleeping car (recentl

although not specially, built), incorporated into the rake for publicity purposes. However, the remaining vehicles ordered for this second generation of the train were not destined to enter service before the outbreak of World War II. In 1940 construction of the remaining vehicles was suspended, while the existing stock remained marooned in the USA. By 1944, as recounted by Essery and Jenkinson, the chief mechanical engineer, C. E. Fairburn, applied for permission to complete the remainder of this stillborn generation of the train. Twenty-five partially-completed coaches existed, while the final number, including those returned from across the Atlantic, came to twenty-nine. Most of these were to see some service on the LMS system in what remained of that company's life before nationalisation on 1 January 1948, also in BR days. However, as the 1939–46 marque of Coronation Scot coaches did not operate as a streamlined train service, they will not be considered further, except to note in passing their construction and decor.

The new stock was largely articulated, with the apparent original proposal that the first set should be made up of three triplets and a single coach. This appears to have been modified down to articulated twins with a single coach making up an odd number. One addition was the

existence of a cocktail bar whose decor seems to have met with approval, Brian Haresnape describing it as 'Hollywood cinema' in style. It was officially described as 'a symphony in red white and blue'.

* * *

The first public announcement about the LMS entry into the world of streamlined expresses came at the 14th annual general meeting of the company in London on 26 February 1937. Chairman Sir Josiah Stamp informed stockholders of 'a new and special London–Glasgow service each way leaving at about 1.30pm, stopping at Carlisle only'. He was quick to insist that there would be no race with the LNER, whose new London–Edinburgh service was already announced for the following summer, and the lack of any competition on the matter of speed was soon to be underlined by the revelation that the

Even on a cloudy day, the livery of No 6221 *Princess Elizabeth* positively gleams as the Coronation Scot heads southwards on Shap in the first year of the train's operation. This locomotive was the only streamlined member of the class to carry successively blue, red, and black liveries before being destreamlined. *(RAS Marketing)*

Streamlined trains on the LNER were timetabled uphill almost as fast as on the down stretches. This did not seem to apply on the LMS, certainly not as far as the Carnforth–Shap timing was concerned, and there were often improvements on timetable on this section. No 6222 *Queen Mary* is pictured on Shap in 1937.   (RAS Marketing)

Euston–Glasgow (Central) schedule was to be no less than 6½ hours for the 401 miles.

This was still above a 60 mph average over a considerable distance but was nevertheless disappointing, given that a non-streamlined engine had hustled an eight-coach load between the two cities in some 45 minutes *less* the previous November. No wonder Cecil J. Allen described the new schedule as an 'anti-climax' and insisted on paying more attention, in his monthly magazine articles assessing locomotive performance, to the LNER's streamlined trains, with their more demanding timings. In defence of the LMS, it has to be said that its West Coast main line was more hilly than the rival East Coast route; the twin summits of Shap and Beattock presented more formidable obstacles than anything faced by Gresley's A4s. On the other hand, as Gresley himself pointed out

at a public meeting around this time, one of the outstanding advantages of streamlined rolling stock was the possibility of timetabling uphill stretches at hitherto impracticable speeds, and the work of Stanier's non-streamlined No 6201 had certainly proved that even a six-hour schedule might leave something to spare, at least for summer operation.

In May 1937 the LMS announced that its new train would be called the Coronation Scot. The first part of the name obviously marked the coronation of King George VI (which took place on the 12th of the month), while the 'Scot' suffix was standardised nomenclature in line with the Royal Scot and Midday Scot expresses. The livery of Caledonian blue with white speed lines echoed the Scottish theme by employing the pre-Grouping colours of the LMS's biggest constituent company north of the Border, although this does not appear to have been emphasised in the publicity at the time, and the livery was changed without compunction later.

The company showed considerable enterprise in its launching of the new service, inviting the press to visit Crewe Works before the completion of the first Pacific, No 6220 *Coronation*. 'Rolling out' was accompanied by a

press fanfare similar to the unveiling of new airliners nowadays, complemented by a cinema film unashamedly employing Elgar's 'Pomp and Circumstance' march, and very much in contrast to the comparatively secretive birth of the A4 at Doncaster. Drawings of the new locomotive were released to the press to coincide with its first appearance from the Works, in another positive aspect of this impressive public relations exercise.

The entire train was exhibited at Euston for two days during June, and even the technical press did not notice, or at least did not comment on, the fact that most of the stock was not new. The PR launch of the train continued with a film appearance. On Sunday 13 June, the four-track section of line between Llandudno Junction and Colwyn Bay was closed to public traffic and no fewer than three historic trains ran in parallel for the cameras of a film unit mounted on a special train on the fourth line. No 6220 headed its train alongside a typical express of 1911, headed by former LNWR George V class 4–6–0 No 25348, also named *Coronation*, and an 1838 museum piece in the form of Liverpool & Manchester Railway locomotive *Lion* and train. Class 2P 4–4–0 No 695 hauled the special rail-mounted film unit.

The first locomotive and train made a press journey on 29 June, and this one was destined to be almost as famous as *Silver Link*'s debut had been 21 months previously. Not only was a new speed record set up, but the train gained immortal notoriety by nearly demolishing Crewe station!

With the regulator handled by the redoubtable Tom Clarke, hero of the non-stop runs of the previous year, No 6220 set off from Euston on a return trip to Crewe with eight of the 'new' coaches, weighing 263 tons tare. It had been decided beforehand to go for *Silver Link*'s 112mph record down Whitmore bank, omitting a slowing for the nearby water-troughs in the bid. Whitmore was perhaps not an incline in the Shap or Beattock category, nor was it as straight and long as Stoke on the East Coast. It was in fact eight miles at gradients varying from 1 in 177–348, but had the disadvantage of facing northwards – almost straight into Crewe.

No 6220 got off to a good start from Euston, achieving even time by Watford, and went over Whitmore at 85mph. Speed rose inexorably with the incline, the new Pacific showing no reluctance to penetrate triple figures. Soon 113mph or 114mph was achieved – there is a slight contradiction in the records – but Crewe was looming dead ahead. On went the brakes, hard. As luck, or bad management, would have it, the train was pathed to enter platform 3, which involved a reverse bend entry. Flames spurted from the brake-blocks, and spectators blanched at the sight of a streamlined express heading into the Crewe crossovers at what appeared to be a mile a minute.

'The crockery in the dining car crashed. Down we came to 52mph through the curve, with the engine riding like the great lady she is. There wasn't a thing we could do but hold on and let her take it. And take it she did . . .'

This account came from Stanier's assistant, R. A. Riddles, who later headed the BR design teams which produced the Britannia Pacifics and Class 9F 2–10–0s, among other designs. Timing the train were the indefatigable C. J. Allen and O. S. Nock and they remained unconvinced that 113mph was actually exceeded, although Allen did concede that 115mph seemed to be quite feasible until *Coronation* ran out of track, as it were.

The return journey was scheduled for 135 minutes for the 158 miles, but the Pacific made light of this, achieving an arrival inside two hours flat. The 119 minutes for this distance involved an average of 79.7mph, including 72 miles at 88.9mph. Another '100' and a '99' were attained in a southbound run that was to go unequalled for over 20 years, and would not shame a modern electric locomotive. An LMS official was perhaps not stretching matters too far when he told a reporter after the run that No 6220 was in his opinion 'beyond doubt the fastest in the world'.

The new Coronation Scot service, as announced, would start from London and Glasgow simultaneously at 1.30pm, reaching the other city at 8.00pm. The two-minute Carlisle stop allowed for crew changing, the down train (6.13pm to 6.15pm) not picking up, and the up (3.15pm to 3.17pm) not setting down passengers from Glasgow. The section south of Carlisle was shared between crews from Camden and Carlisle (Upperby); north of Carlisle, men from Glasgow (Polmadie) were in

One of the reasons for the LMS and LNER to engage in publicity-seeking exercises such as non-stop runs in the 1920s and record speeds in the 1930s was the existence of an illustrated media. With only two tabloids on the news stands in 1937, the LMS could feel well pleased with the coverage of their 29 June record speed attempt as publicised by the *Daily Sketch*. (*Millbrook House*)

charge, with the engines working through. The departure time was the one traditionally occupied by the Corridor express which later became known as the Midday Scot. The new train took over the London–Glasgow traffic from the existing service, which continued, also serving Edinburgh and the Lancashire cities by taking on and dropping off through coaches at appropriate junctions such as Crewe, Lancaster, Carlisle, and in the southbound direction, Law Junction and Symington.

Ironically, the brochure extolling the virtues of the new express to American visitors, when it later toured the USA, featured the beauties of such Scottish destinations as Edinburgh, Oban, Loch Lomond, and Gleneagles – none of which were actually served by the train! Indeed, any American visitor travelling to north of Glasgow from London by the new service would have to alight at Carlisle and await the arrival of the later Midday Scot

The Coronation Scot streamliner had only days left to run before World War II when this picture was taken of the down service at Cadley in August 1939. Red-liveried Pacific No 6229 *Duchess of Hamilton* (in fact No 6220 *Coronation* in disguise) heads the train, which appears markedly less air-resistant in design, particularly below the frames, than the rival LNER services.   (*RAS Marketing*)

(1.35pm out of Euston) some 80 minutes later and transfer into its Edinburgh section, with connections for more northern destinations being even later. Only Loch Lomond and Edinburgh could be reached from Glasgow (Central), the former by transferring to a suburban service from Central (Low Level), while the Scottish capital was reached by a comparatively slow connecting train via Shotts. The timetabling of this much-vaunted streamlined train is examined critically in the Postscript.

As already observed, the 6½-hour schedule came as a disappointment to the growing number of admirers of Stanier's locomotives. They were perhaps placated temporarily by a syndicated newspaper report on 30 June, the Wednesday prior to the introduction of the service, that

'I am assured by a leading official of the company that the introduction of the 6½ hour service between Glasgow and London is not the end of time-cutting between the two cities. Within the next three years, if the demand for a speedier service should warrant the necessary reorganisation along the main line, a 5½ hours' regular run from Clyde to Thames will be on the railway schedule.'

As we shall see, there was no improvement in timing in the train's 25-month life; in fact the indications are that the company was thinking of improving capacity rather than increasing its speed, had the war not intervened.

Newspaper coverage of the train's introduction was informative, and above all, positive. The LMS stressed that it had carried out a special six-month programme of permanent way work prior to its introduction, with 100 curves, aggregating to 60 miles in length, being realigned and superelevated to make high speeds more comfortable for the passenger.

*   *   *

The simultaneous departures of the up and down Coronation Scot drew considerable crowds to Euston and Glasgow (Central) on Monday 5 July 1937. After years of partisan rivalry between Crewe and Derby in England, and between two of the Scottish constituent companies, the LMS had at last created a *new* totem for all company employees to identify with. It was perfectly obvious on the LNER that professional railwaymen enjoyed a dash of imagination in the planning and operation of express services, such as the non-stop Flying Scotsman and the later streamliners. Here at last was the LMS's reply, and a distinctive looking one it was, too.

Not too surprisingly, both trains reached their destinations ahead of time, the up service two minutes early, hauled by No 6221 *Queen Elizabeth*. The locomotive was crewed by David Kerr and H. Shelden from Glasgow to Carlisle, and by John Curran and H. Scott southwards. The newspapers credit the northern crew with averaging 70mph from Glasgow to Beattock (including more than 20 miles of gradual hill-climbing), and an average of 82mph from Beattock to Lockerbie, probably from Beattock summit. The down train was greeted at Central, four minutes early, by Sir Josiah Stamp. The locomotive was presumably No 6220, its driver when Glasgow was reached being Kerr, working back on the down service. Both locomotives were based at the London depot of Camden; indeed, up until the opening of the war, all the streamlined Pacifics were allocated there when new.

From the outset of their careers, the Princess Coronation Pacifics were intended to haul general expresses as well as the 'streamliner'. Here No 6224 *Princess Alexandra* climbs from Edge Hill to Wavertree Junction with a Liverpool (Lime Street)–London (Euston) express sometime in 1938.   (*Millbrook House*)

The first passenger to purchase a reservation ticket for the up train was one Arthur Findlay, a Glaswegian now living in Essex. He had left home at 9.45pm the previous evening, travelled overnight to Glasgow, and was now returning, after a morning's meetings, with a scheduled arrival time of 9.00pm on his own doorstep. Perhaps he was too polite to tell the press, when interviewed, that a 4.00pm departure would have suited him as a businessman even better, giving him most of the working day in Glasgow on a trip for which he had sacrificed a night's sleep at home.

It all seems fairly routine to us nowadays, when air travel has made Britain so much smaller, but the darker aspect behind Mr Findlay's words was the fact that this kind of inter-city travel should have been available decades before. The wretched 1896 agreement between East and West Coast companies had required that services between London and Edinburgh/Glasgow should not accomplish the journey in less than 8¼ hours. This was a cartel operating against the public interest, and it is surprising that the LMS and LNER continued it after they came into existence in 1923. Even the LNER's non-stop service was scheduled for a 48mph average between Edinburgh and London in the summers between 1928–31 inclusive, with its relief train keeping the same schedule, but with four stops.

Not until 1932 was this insane agreement terminated – as it could have been years before. Its original intention had been to prevent racing, but this could have been achieved by a mutual agreement assigning Glasgow as a primary destination for the West Coast companies and the later LMS, and Edinburgh as a secondary one with an agreed upper time 'limit'. This would be reversed for the East Coast interests. In other words, the West would be allowed Glasgow as its 'territory', but would have to ensure that connections or through sections to Edinburgh took no less than a specified timing. The public seemed to have been unaware of this cartel, and Lord Monkswell's was a lone voice in the wilderness. This was a sad comment on the lack of interest in the operation of Britain's railways; this ignorance created a climate of tolerance towards the LNER and LMS offering less than

a first-class service. The disappointing 6½-hour schedule of the Coronation Scot, when a faster, perhaps a non-stop, service was technically feasible and commercially desirable, was but a legacy of the treaty of 1896. After all, 6½ hours was such an improvement . . .

* * *

From the three years of streamlined running on the West Coast main line, 1937–39, there are disappointingly few records of high-speed performances, particularly when compared to the mercurial dashes on the rival East Coast. Many contemporary observers believed that the 6½-hour schedule might be accelerated when operating experience had been gained, although the construction of the 1939 'generation' of Coronation Scot rolling stock, intended as a ten-coach rake, suggested that the company was going for greater future passenger capacity in preference to higher average speed.

The service operated five days a week, with one of the sets making a weekend return to the North Wales coast, the scene of its film début, by forming a down Euston–Llandudno express on summer Saturdays in 1938, and back on a Sunday service. More Saturday employment was soon found for one of the streamlined sets by taking out one of its kitchen cars, adding normal stock, and sending it out on the down Midday Scot with a Sunday return. While undoubtedly an economical use of vehicles, all this hardly added to the exclusivity of the Coronation Scot image, and Saturday operation of the train could surely have been considered, particularly since it was operating in a recognised midday passenger channel and was not specifically catering for business travellers.

As might be expected, punctuality on the service was good, with every station arrival in September 1937 – all 88 of them – being early or on time. No 6220 was dynamometer-tested on down and up journeys in November 1937, the test coach making up a ten-coach assembly grossing about 350 tons. This was no problem for the Pacific, which breasted Shap at 42mph, and Beattock at 39mph. Going south, the latter summit, with its long but gradual climb from the north, was crossed at 57mph. Coal consumption worked out at 39.2 lb/mile. One writer, J. F. Clay, has suggested that during 1937–39 'there were occasions when the coal did not last out', citing an instance when coal was exhausted on an up journey as far from the London destination as Nuneaton. More evidence of this would be interesting, as the

November return journey just mentioned appeared to have involved consuming little more than seven tons of coal overall (70 per cent of tender capacity), and that with a heavier than normal load.

The lack of challenge presented to Stanier's locomotives was doubly disappointing considering a February 1939 test run where an unstreamlined member of the class, No 6234 *Duchess of Abercorn* hauled a Crewe–Glasgow train of 610 tons over the northern summits with considerable élan. The 31.4 miles from Carnforth to Shap summit were covered in 33 minutes 20 seconds, well inside the Coronation Scot schedule, but with twice the load. Coming south, 60mph was recorded at Beattock summit and an estimated 3,333hp generated. The fireman deserved as much credit for this as the designer! It all served to underline the disappointing nature of the Coronation Scot scheduling; indeed, on one occasion when No 6220 made up time in a 135 minute dash from Crewe to Euston, the average speed would have made the train late by LNER streamlined schedules south of York!

As already observed, the timing of the new LMS express was not challenging enough to excite the same attention from railway journalists that the LNER streamliners received, but two northbound runs which were recorded early in the train's short history of service indicated varying degrees of success in operating the streamliner. On one journey the doyen of the class of Pacifics was into Carlisle slightly early but some ten minutes to the good in net terms. This was despite losing 85 seconds for an emergency stop at Rugby to clear a sander, and being 3½ minutes late at Carnforth. However, a good climb to Shap summit, passed at 36mph, made up the arrears. On the second run, some inconsistency in driving technique was discernible, the early part of the journey including two 'nineties', but a slackening off

Lower semaphore signals frame No 6220 *Coronation* as it climbs towards Wavertree on a Liverpool (Lime Street)–London (Euston) express in 1938. Like their counterparts on the East Coast, the drivers of West Coast streamlined trains had to rely on 19th century signalling methods.   (*Millbrook House*)

thereafter, with Preston passed 2¼ minutes late. Again the northern hills had no terrors for the locomotive, this time No 6221, and Carlisle was reached punctually.

Published logs of the northern part of the journey of the train suggested sound but unspectacular timekeeping. On one occasion No 6220 attained Beattock summit, including twelve miles of climbing, nearly ten of them at around 1 in 80, in 46.5 minutes for the 49.7 miles from Carlisle. After this commendable effort, no hard running was required down the Clyde valley to ensure a punctual arrival at Glasgow. On another run, No 6221 ran hard northwards down from Beattock summit, but met such signal delays as to be six minutes late into Central.

One magazine correspondent argued in 1938 that the LMS was sensibly timing the train with something to spare in its schedule to allow for the kind of checks inevitable in such a complex rail system. The 100 per cent punctuality figures recorded in September 1937 certainly seemed to bear this out, although the writer conceded that this peak of performance had not been repeated subsequently.

One of eleven sets of water-troughs on the West Coast main line, Dillicar near Tebay, offers sustenance to No 6224 *Princess Alexandra* on the up Coronation on 22 July 1938. *(Gresley Society)*

In contrast, the LNER operated on the threshold of practicable performance with its Coronation express, whose timing south of Newcastle was even faster than that of the Silver Jubilee and was equally unprecedented north of the Tyne. Yet a subsequent chapter will show that the Coronation enjoyed a very good 77 per cent minimum punctuality record in all the samples this author has examined. Perhaps operating on the very edge of what was practicable for man and machine inspired train crews to make special performances commonplace? The LMS, a company which badly needed some kind of emblem for its various constituent companies to rally round, should have looked at this aspect of the matter a little harder.

The LNER's more enterprising venture into streamlined train services encountered a positive, almost enthusiastic, response from footplate crews – despite the disappointing lack of proper training offered them. Skilled workmen during Britain's industrial age were always open to new techniques and challenges, provided that they were given appropriate tools for the job. On the East Coast, the A4 was that tool. On the West, there was also a new class of locomotives built for high speed but no resulting challenge for the crews to aim at. How can one avoid indicting the LMS board and management of a

charge of spinelessness, of being quite unworthy of the railway staff and footplatemen they employed?

* * *

As already mentioned the new Pacifics were provided with an unprecedented ten-ton supply of coal, complete with steam-powered pusher to move the supply towards the fireman when required. Water provision was however less generous, with only 80 per cent of the A4's 5,000 gallon supply, despite having to accomplish a journey eight miles longer, and with no time available for taking water during the two-minute Carlisle stop.

Obviously the operation of the Coronation Scot would have been impossible if there had been no water-troughs, but it was in fact one of the LMS's major constituent companies, the London & North Western Railway, which had pioneered these features as far back as 1860. No fewer than eleven sets now existed between Euston and Glasgow Central, two sets being specially laid by the LMS in Scotland, on the former Caledonian section of the West Coast main line. Their location, compared to six on the East Coast main line, are shown opposite in the accompanying scaled diagram.

The LMS made a generous provision compared to that of water troughs on the rival East Coast main line. Footplate crews on the latter had to run from Scrooby, south of Doncaster, 247 miles to Edinburgh with only two sets of troughs, while Wiske Moor and Lucker were not far short of 100 miles apart. If one considers that concern about water provision could have inhibited a crew's performance in running hard, the absence of such a problem on the west coast meant that there really was no justification here for the rather slothful Coronation Scot schedule of 6½ hours.

Apart from its five-days-a-week duty, the Coronation Scot undertook an unusual royal function on 5 November of its first year. King Boris of Bulgaria, an inveterate railway enthusiast, was treated to a footplate run on No 6220 with a streamlined train set (presumably the spare one, since this was a Friday) on a special run from Euston to Bletchley and back. The 46.7 mile run was accomplished in 45 minutes, with a maximum speed of 88mph; for the sake of variety, Royal Scot class No 6145 made the return journey in 51 minutes. Since there is no record of the King sampling LNER streamlined operations, it is conceivable that the LMS propaganda had had international appeal sufficient to eclipse the LNER star – it

West Coast main line
GLASGOW (Central)

West Coast main line	miles	East Coast main line
GLASGOW (Central)	400 miles	EDINBURGH (Waverley)
32		
369 CARSTAIRS		
		73
63	350 miles	
306 FLORISTON		LUCKER 319
	300 miles	
45		
		97
261 TEBAY		
27	250 miles	
234 HEST BANK		
17		
217 GARSTANG		WISKE MOOR 222
39	200 miles	
		76
178 PRESTON BROOK		
30		
148 WHITMORE	150 miles	SCROOBY 146
36		24
		MUSKHAM 122
112 TAMWORTH		
29	100 miles	43
83 RUGBY		WERRINGTON 79
30		
53 WOLVERTON		52
38	50 miles	
		LANGLEY 27
15 BUSHEY		miles
miles		

Euston   LONDON   King's Cross
West Coast main line   East Coast main line

certainly did in the USA. Unfortunately, royal biographers tend not to pay much attention to such matters, so it seems unlikely if we will ever know if the Bulgarian monarch, who died mysteriously after a visit to Hitler in 1943, rated Crewe above Doncaster!

Three days later, the Scot experienced another out-of-the-ordinary event when it was diverted on to the Settle and Carlisle line. With its usual route blocked at Milnthorpe, the up service on 8 November 1937 had its train engine, No 6221, replaced at Carlisle by Jubilee class No 5604 *Ceylon*, which took the streamliner through the Pennines, regaining its normal route after travelling by Hellifield and Blackburn.

In 1938 the LMS revealed that the latest streamlined locomotives for the Coronation Scot and other major services would be painted red, or more exactly crimson lake, with gold speed lines, each band being lined with a ½in black 'shadow'. Some repainting of the original five took place, but the reader can be forgiven for finding all this assortment of liveries somewhat confusing. Presumably the abandonment of Caledonian blue in preference for crimson was to eliminate the colour clash of a blue engine hauling a non-streamlined train. Only one of the original five Pacifics, No 6221, carried all three liveries

(listed below) by the end of the war, the other four going directly from blue to black. The *original* colours of the streamlined Princess Coronation (Duchess) Pacifics were as follows:

6220–4	Blue with silver lines.
6225–9	Crimson lake with gold.
6235–44	Crimson lake with gold.
6245–8	Unlined black.

(More details of this class in appendix).

The second generation of passenger rolling-stock for the Coronation Scot was, as we have seen, crimson and gold, and this was destined to be exhibited at the New York's World Fair in 1939. Eight coaches including a First sleeping car made up the train itself, with No 6220 the locomotive. In fact the latest Pacific was sent, No 6229, exchanging name and number with the doyen of the class, and a headlight and bell were fixed to this changeling.

American citizens were privileged to see, as here at East Chatham, New York State, the combination of Princess Coronation Pacific (actually No 6229 'posing' as 6220) and specially-built Coronation Scot rolling stock — something never seen in the UK. The legally necessary headlight and bell are particularly noticeable.   (*RAS Marketing*)

Locomotive and coaches were worked separately as two trains to Southampton via Willesden and Eastleigh for shipping on the MS *Belpamela* on 20 January. Driver Bishop and Fireman Cassell made up the crew, along with an unnamed relief fireman. The locomotive was pictured in many a national newspaper being lowered into the ship's hold, while the less fortunate coaches had to endure the Atlantic crossing in midwinter as deck cargo, being specially waxed for protection from salt and wind. They would certainly need such treatment, the ship being delayed nearly a week by storms in mid-ocean.

The outbreak of war in September 1939 (as far as Europe was concerned) marooned the Coronation Scot in the USA, the locomotive not being able to return until 1942, the coaches having to remain overseas until the end of the war. The real No 6220 ran as 6229 for another three years, and it was this engine that was involved in one of the few breakdowns of the Coronation Scot, on 20 July 1939.

This happened at Tring, where the Pacific had to come off the up train with an overheated axlebox. Fowler-designed 2–6–4 tank No 2354 was promoted to take over, covering the 31.7 miles on to Euston in 34 minutes start-to-stop, with driver Grives at the regulator. A curious feature of this report was that the Pacific driver stayed with his crippled engine instead of carrying on with the company's most important train.

The LMS exhibition train of 1939 approaches Hartford (USA) behind the 'changeling' No 6220. The rolling stock, with its fairings almost down to rail level, looks far superior to the coaches first provided for the Coronation Scot service two years before.   (*RAS Marketing*)

Below: Although not aesthetically pleasing, black-liveried No 6245 *City of London*, would have offered the 1943 passenger the impression of enormous power. (*National Railway Museum*)

6 LNER – THE CORONATION

'NEVER SO FAR, SO FAST, SO PUNCTUALLY'

Early in 1936 the technical press carried details of new locomotive construction by the LNER, to include no fewer than 17 Pacifics similar to *Silver Link*. These would be constructed with assistance from a government guaranteed loan, which may possibly explain why they took so long to appear. The first, No 4482 *Golden Eagle*, was not outshopped until December, but it was the seventh of the class which was the first to be allocated to a particular service – and a new one at that – the Coronation.

The LNER had not been slow to emphasise that it planned to extend its Silver Jubilee type service over an even longer distance. London to Aberdeen, 524 miles, was considered the obvious course for a new 'streamliner', and provisional times were drawn up at a planning meeting on 14 July 1936. The down train would leave King's Cross at 12.15pm, pause in Newcastle from 4.10pm to 4.15pm (268 miles in 235 minutes; a five-minute acceleration on the timing of the Silver Jubilee), arrive at Edinburgh two hours later, where there would be a 15 minute stop, Aberdeen being reached in another 2¾ hours – nine hours flat from London. The up train would leave at 9.15am and keep to a similar schedule. North of Edinburgh there would be stops at Kirkcaldy, Arbroath and Montrose, the last of these being virtually unavoidable, for operational reasons. Apart from the fastest-ever time south of Newcastle, there would also be a very fast timing north of Edinburgh, where gradients, sharp curves, and mining subsidences, not to mention a stretch of single-line near Montrose, were perennial problems for express operations.

This was a bold dream, particularly since no train had ever been scheduled to such timings over any part of the intended route, or had actually run so fast north of Newcastle, apart from the famous Races to the North. As

The first of the second batch of A4s, No 4482 *Golden Eagle*, is seen at Great Ponton on a northbound general passenger duty not long after construction in 1936. As detailed in the text, a youthful passenger timed this engine at 107mph on the Coronation express in 1939, but the crew disagreed, claiming 110mph!   (*RAS Marketing*)

an experiment, it was decided to operate the spare Gateshead A4, No 2511 *Silver King*, north from Newcastle on the Silver Jubilee set plus dynamometer car, on Saturday 26 September 1936. Speed restrictions were specially eased at three locations for the A4 and its 255 ton train, and with a Gateshead crew, Edinburgh was reached three minutes early, in 117 minutes. Southwards another minute was saved, proving the practicality of the schedule.

However, the most interesting part of the run was the climbing at no speed lower than 68mph of Cockburnspath bank (four miles at 1 in 96) on the return journey. In his Presidential address to the Institution of Mechanical

Engineers in the following October, the recently-knighted Sir Nigel Gresley announced that an estimated 2,600hp had been generated on the climb, a record at that time for a British express locomotive.

The LNER's Scottish area manager, George Mills, cabled Wedgwood on 30 September 1936 acknowledging the latter's memo (mentioned in Chapter 4 on the

A unique shot of the Silver Jubilee *north* of Newcastle. No 2511 *Silver King* heads northwards through Morpeth with the empty train set, plus a dynamometer car, while establishing that a two-hour service between Newcastle and Edinburgh was feasible. Saturday 26 September 1936 was the date. *(National Railway Museum)*

Silver Jubilee) concerning the re-positioning and, where necessary, the duplication of distant signals, and commented that it had no immediate relevance to his area – a somewhat short-sighted view, one might think, given the plans then being mooted for an Anglo-Scottish streamlined train. However, Mills advised Wedgwood that some stretches of Scottish line were already being signalled 'several sections in advance', giving as an example the 5½ miles between Monktonhall Junction and Edinburgh (Waverley).

Less well known than the 1936 'dress rehearsal' involving *Silver King* hauling the Jubilee stock between Newcastle and Edinburgh was a brake trial held by the LNER Scottish Area on Sunday 3 November 1935. Its purpose was to test whether there was a safe distance margin between the sighting of a distant signal at caution and stopping dead at the following home signal. In this it had anticipated Wedgwood's September 1936 memo listing the number of inadequately spaced distant signals on the former GNR, GER, and GCR, and making Wedgwood's omission of NER and NBR figures somewhat surprising. North of the Border there was certainly a problem in this respect.

Hauled by A1 No 2566 *Ladas*, a 250 ton rake of six coaches and two bogie vans was scheduled to be taken from Cowlairs (Glasgow) to Grantshouse, the summit of Cockburnspath bank on the East Coast main line. The overall timing was not particularly high; indeed, the locomotive ran round its train at Haymarket on the up journey and, incongruously, proceeded tender-first on to the East Coast main line. This suggests that the main objective of the trip was to test braking distances on the

return journey down Cockburnspath bank and on the practically level Edinburgh (Waverley)–Glasgow (Queen Street) section, where speeds could be expected to be high. To facilitate this, in the down direction, the bogie vans were detached at Waverley, reducing the tare load to 200 tons. It is worth recording the results as this author does not recall their being recorded in book form before, and they sum up the problems faced by LNER officials planning to run high-speed trains on a system designed to accommodate every type of traffic from a coal train at near walking pace to a luxury express.

'Overshoots' were recorded as follows at five out of six locations:

Location	Speed (mph)	Overshoot (ft)	Braking time to stop (secs)
Up			
Falkirk High	74	585	46.5
Linlithgow	80	250	46.5
Down			
Dunbar (East)	80–85	752	51.0
Linlithgow	78	419	46.0
Dullatur	72	50	51.5

One suspects that these findings were somewhat imprecise as they do not appear to indicate if the driver was instructed to apply the brake when the distant was first sighted or actually reached – probably the latter, as normal conditions were being simulated. Interestingly, *Ladas* was able to bring its train screeching to a halt within the distant-home length after descending Cockburnspath bank at 74mph, pulling up within 50 seconds of braking. This was probably because the signal placings anticipated high speeds down the bank, whereas at Dunbar, where speed was even higher on this occasion, a considerable 'overshoot' resulted. The archival papers documenting the trial do not indicate what if any signal replacement operations took place as a result. Nor do they mention the possibility of streamlined operations west of Edinburgh, though such a proposition was reasonable.

According to Norman Newsome, Gresley's assistant, the original plan for the Coronation was to follow closely that so successful with the Silver Jubilee, transporting 200 passengers in a formation which would include restaurant

Roses and a thistle adorn the internal bulkhead of one of the Coronation observation cars, viewed from the luggage area. The cars in fact ran for less than half of the train's life. *(National Railway Museum)*

cars. Newsome and his colleague Leslie Nicholson apparently worked until late in the night on draft plans for the rolling stock – having been asked to start this work at three o'clock one afternoon – only to find that their drawings were rejected, as was a later draft. The decision was made to serve meals at the passengers' seats, replacing the two restaurant cars with two kitchen cars. 'We want to go one better than the Pullman', Gresley was reported as saying. Four articulated twin cars would make up a basic rake of eight vehicles.

A novelty to be included in the new train was an observation car to bring up the rear and allow an all-round view. This had been part of Bel Geddes' vision for a streamlined train, and was put into service in Manchuria on the Asia Express and in the USA on the Hiawatha. These were by no means 'firsts'. Indeed, the Caledonian Railway had entertained its Pullman passengers on the Oban line with backward-looking views of Highland scenery from the *Maid of Morven* car from about 1914. However, Gresley's car was to have a 'beaver tail' shape designed to destroy any vacuum forming at the back of the train, thus eliminating air resistance. Gresley appears to have first revealed details of wind tunnel research on this concept at an Institution of Mechanical Engineers meeting in November 1936, although it does not seem to have attracted comment at that stage. Ironically, thanks to a world war and some unimaginative management, Gresley's observation cars were destined to spend more time plying lines in the Western Highlands, like their Caledonian predecessor, than they were ever to do on the East Coast main line.

* * *

While the Silver Jubilee constituted a single seven- (later eight-) coach set, the Coronation went into service with no fewer than three sets. One of these, not carrying lettering, was used as a spare for all three streamlined services operated by the company. Two sets were required for the Coronation, as it departed from King's Cross at 4.00pm and Edinburgh Waverley at 4.30pm on its unprecedentedly fast six-hour journey to the other terminus.

The same constructional details – steel body panels on a teak frame – applied, although, perhaps not surprisingly, more sound insulation was provided. Asbestos acoustic blankets were inserted in the roof spaces and in the bodysides and underframes.

Unlike the Jubilee, with its First class compartments, the Coronation was entirely centre-gangwayed, although every bay in First class and every second bay in Third, was divided into compartments, effectively 'slicing-up' the train. All seats (48 First, 168 Third) were reservable, those in First being movable armchairs. The upholstery was described as 'uncut fawn moquette'; the carpets were green, and the interior walls were decorated in two shades of grey-green 'Rexine' separated by a fretted trim. The overall effect was not perhaps to everyone's taste; the late Brian Haresnape commented that the decor 'seemed more like a boudoir than a railway carriage'.

Lavatories were positioned at the extreme ends of each car, so that passengers did not have to pass them when entering the train and making their way to their seats. Steam heating was used to warm the water in winter, and electrical power in summer. The latter source of heating combined with electrical power for the cookers and refrigerators to place certain constraints on the operation of the train. Some railwaymen believed that the number of axle-driven alternators effectively added to the drag of the stock, while dynamo belts working loose were a recurring feature, if not an endemic one, on the service.

The internal colour scheme was very much in contrast to the blue theme of the train's exterior. Advised by the British Colour Council, the LNER chose Marlborough blue for above the train's 'waist' (the bottom of the window line), and darker Garter blue for below. Stainless steel was used for the trim lines and for the lettering – which was 6in Gill Sans for the word Coronation and 4in for the coach numbers. Early publicity photographs of the train reveal that panels on the leading brake and at the corridor end of the observation car, carried the insignia of England (three lions couchant) and Scotland (a single lion rampant) respectively. These did not appear on the service train – perhaps their use was not cleared with the College of Heralds and Lord Lyon? The roofs were spray-painted aluminium, while the entire underframes were completely black.

Two odd characteristics of the air conditioning were that First class passengers were subjected to knee-level draughts, until alterations could be effected, and warm air worked backwards through to the rear of the train. F. A. S. Brown, Gresley's biographer, believed that this was because of the inertia effect of high speed on warm air.

The rear of the train of course comprised the Observation Car, its sixteen seats available to all passengers on

payment of 1s (5p) for an hour's use viewing through the rear Perspex panels, which had been specially shaped by ICI. The LNER's Eric Bannister believed that dust and grit was attracted to the perspex 'as if by magic'. The coach was single-ended and had to be turned at the end of each journey, either on a turntable or on a triangular junction. With a luggage section incorporated into the trainward end of the vehicle (Newsome records that it was intended to be converted into a cocktail bar if thought necessary), extra ballasting was necessary at the rear end of the coach to compensate for this imbalance. The introduction of the car effectively duplicated 16 of the 216 seats in the train and added an extra 30 tons to the tare weight of the train without remuneration, except the mere £4 that was the maximum which could be collected in a single journey.

In his book on Gresley's coaching-stock (see Bibliography), Michael Harris sagely points out: 'Railway coach interior design is either of the moment or intended to remain acceptable over a longer period. The Coronation was fashionable in that sense, but criticism must be levelled at detail . . .' Presumably Mr Harris meant that the trains came into the former category; certainly it is hard for even the least artistic eye to reconcile the attractive but cold exterior in blue with the softer greys, greens and fawn internally.

Special arrangements were made for the stabling and cleaning of the stock after use. It may seem incredible to us in our age of easily cleaned surfaces, but the exterior of the Coronation rolling stock was cleaned after every journey by hand. On arrival at King's Cross the empty stock was taken to Wellington sidings where it was inspected and received any necessary repairs until 6.00am, when cleaning began. Good old-fashioned soap flakes and water were used on the coach exteriors, these then being leathered and polished. N1 0–6–2T No 4586 was kept specially clean for taking the stock to and from the terminus whenever possible. At King's Cross the observation car was turned by turntable, while at the Edinburgh end Craigentinny sidings was the site for the stock's cleaning and preparation, the observation car being turned on the nearby Niddrie triangle.

* * *

The 12.15pm down and 9.15am up departure times were not finalised, Sir Ralph Wedgwood overruling the Superintendents and Passenger Managers Committee on the grounds that later departure times – 4.00pm down and 4.30pm up – would suit travelling businessmen better. Unfortunately for the LNER, this proved to be wishful thinking, certainly in the case of the down journey. As for point-to-point timings, a press briefing document issued by the LNER in the summer of 1937 stressed the high speeds required going uphill, as well as detailing some of the more spectacular intermediate timings scheduled. Shortly before the train's introduction, Gresley had publicly pointed out that, over a distance downhill of 15 miles (roughly the length of Stoke Bank), increasing train speed from 60mph to 90mph only saved five minutes, 'but to increase uphill running speed from thirty to sixty saves fifteen minutes'.

In the down direction, the 27 miles from Hitchin to Huntingdon was required to be run by the Coronation in 19 minutes pass-to-pass (85mph), and the largely uphill Peterborough–Grantham section, Stoke Bank included, in 24 minutes (72.7mph for 29 miles pass-to-pass). York was reached at 6.37pm in 157 minutes from London, an average only a shade below 72mph. This had to be achieved with a load 40 per cent heavier than that of the Silver Jubilee. The speed requirement north of York was easier by some 10mph, although there was no scope for loitering between York and Darlington on the former NER 'racing ground' – forty-one minutes start to pass for 44 miles, while the 11.5 miles from Dunbar to Drem required 72.6mph. After the timetable was tightened in March 1938 to include a Newcastle stop in the down direction, some nine minutes was effectively docked from this timing, making the train a real operational challenge.

The up Coronation required an average of 62.4mph between Edinburgh and Newcastle and 68mph thence to King's Cross. It was allowed a minute less on the 'racing ground', with 74.4mph having to be averaged between Grantham and Peterborough, and 77mph between Huntingdon and Hitchin. That there was something to spare in the timing for the former NER stretch was evidenced as early as 24 August 1937 when an A4 on the up service made up five minutes of lateness between leaving Newcastle and passing Shaftholme Junction, just north of Doncaster. By March of the following year, some adjustments had been made, with five minutes effectively being 'transferred' from the schedule north of York to south of there. In other words, the up train now passed through the minster city at 7.48pm instead of at 7.53pm, leaving 162 minutes for the remaining 188 miles. This indicated increased confidence in the train's ability to stop

easily if checked in the colour-light sections north of York.

How Gresley's A4s dealt with the challenge of such protractedly high speeds over the near 400 miles distance will be examined later.

In spotless condition, No 4491 Commonwealth of Australia *is seen on Cockburnspath bank with the Coronation, possibly on the first up run, early in July 1937. (RAS Marketing)*

* * *

To launch the new service, the LNER planned two press trips. The first of them is the only one which is mentioned in the usual histories of LNER operations, consisting of a return journey between King's Cross and Grantham. The date was 30 June 1937 with No 4489 *Dominion of Canada.* The previous day had seen the LMS reach 114mph with its new Princess Coronation Pacific, and very nearly demolish the south end of Crewe station into the bargain! With a 15 mile downhill stretch (Stoke bank) and 21 months of high speed experience, the LNER management had every reason to believe that the record could be wrested back. Before the train had set off, chief general manager Ralph Wedgwood had once again stressed that this was an introduction to a regular service and not a once-off record breaker, but commented 'our drivers are confident that they could do 120mph with these engines, but we do not encourage them to try'.

In fact, 109mph was the maximum obtained. Cecil J. Allen, having survived the near-debacle at Crewe, believed that the A4 chosen for the LNER's reply was not one of King's Cross's best, although that could hardly have been known to the operating authorities so soon after its appearance.

The second press trip was the more interesting, not least because it is less well known. The Scottish press were invited to sample one of the new sets, hauled by No 4491 *Commonwealth of Australia,* in a return journey between Edinburgh and Newcastle on Friday 2 July 1937. *The Scotsman*'s representative reported that this was probably the fastest ever invasion of England by the Scots, and he was not far wrong. After leaving Waverley at 11.15am, the special apparently was into Newcastle Central at 1.07pm. This gave the remarkable time of 112 minutes for a start-to-stop southward journey of 124.5 miles, and would undoubtedly constitute a record at the time if we knew whether the correspondent was keeping

Almost alone at its King's Cross platform, No 4489 *Dominion of Canada*, carries its new nameplates unveiled on 15 June 1937, three weeks before the new Coronation service was due to begin. In the following year this locomotive received a bell donated by the Canadian Pacific Railway. (*RAS Marketing*)

his own times, or reading from station clocks. However, it could hardly have been anything but fast, with 'nearly 60mph' maintained up the four miles of Cockburnspath bank and 86mph between Reston and Ayton. Coming back in a reported 114 minutes, 93mph was attained at Goswick. Driver John Binnie was at the regulator, with Oliver Bulleid one of the senior staff in the train. Obviously, the Great Northern main line was not the only place where fast running could be attained.

*　*　*

Monday 5 July was a great day for railway enthusiasts in London. After seeing off the first down Coronation Scot from Euston, they would have time for a late lunch before strolling along to King's Cross to witness the first departure of the new Coronation on the LNER at 4.00pm. By all accounts, some two thousand people took the opportunity to do this, emptying King's Cross platform ticket machines of their entire stocks and practically besieging No 4491 *Commonwealth of Australia*, Driver Dron and Fireman Charlton of Gateshead, and their new train, complete with observation car.

Present, and no doubt jostled by the crowd, were the chief general manager, Ralph Wedgwood, and the chief mechanical engineer, Sir Nigel Gresley, the latter travelling on the train with the chairman, William Whitelaw. They saw the 4.00pm for Newcastle start almost simultaneously from platform 10 with the new streamliner from platform 5, and this may have given one or other of them the idea of re-enacting such an event specially for the press, as was done later that month, on the 20th. Incidentally, while we may look back on streamlined steam-powered trains as very much a product of the 1930s, it is pertinent to record that the northbound Coronation was televised by the BBC passing Alexandra

Cabside detail from No 4490 *Empire of India*, a locomotive which began its working life at King's Cross, but spent most of its time at Haymarket. It ran out of coal at Hitchin on one southbound Coronation journey, prompting the removal of streamline fairings from the A4 tender to increase coal capacity. (*RAS Marketing*)

Palace. While this was hardly an outside broadcast in the sense we know nowadays, it was nevertheless a link with our own times.

A brilliant run ensued, timed by the indefatigable Cecil J. Allen. Peterborough was passed only 80 seconds over the even hour, Grantham after less than another 24 minutes 'over the hill', and Doncaster in only 125 minutes 11 seconds. York was reached in the excellent time of 155 minutes 36 seconds, this with a load Mr Allen gave as 330 tons – 40 per cent more than the Silver Jubilee at that time. Charles Brown, chief civil engineer, was a fellow-passenger and frequently made his way to Allen's seat to discover what speeds were being attained (and, no doubt, whether restrictions were being observed). Another Gateshead crew (Messrs Hutchinson and Jobling) took over at York for the second half of the journey, and CJA later found occasion to complain that the Scottish permanent way was in the same kind of unsuitable state of preparation for high-speed running as the former GNR line had been in 1935. Reporting a remarkable 94mph 'below Innerwick', he claimed he had to dodge luggage cannonading off the racks! Perhaps the LNER could profitably have copied the LMS in easing its curves prior to introducing the new service.

Thirty minutes after the down train steamed out of King's Cross, No 4489 *Dominion of Canada* was setting off with the up streamliner, deliberately timed later than the down in order to improve connections from points north and west of Edinburgh. The city's Lord Provost made a short speech, comparing this 'royal' departure with a genuinely royal arrival that morning – King George VI and Queen Elizabeth (later the Queen Mother) had just begun their first visit to the Scottish capital since their accession, via their preferred Edinburgh station, Princes Street. This visit was unfortunately to rob the LNER's new train of much of its impact as far as the Scottish newspapers were concerned.

The first up Coronation was headed by No 4489 *Dominion of Canada*, and the engine is here seen on the GN section on an unknown date. This locomotive reached 109mph on a press trip before the introduction of the service. (*W. E. Boyd collection*)

At 4.30pm the A4 headed out of Waverley for the Calton tunnels, driven by Daniel Maguire and not John Binnie as reported in the *LNER Magazine* and the usually authoritative RCTS history of the LNER's locomotives, (see the Bibliography). Of the latter, it has to be said that this gives the date of the Coronation's introduction as 3 July – a Saturday. Maguire was a reluctant interviewee for BBC radio, before the Lord Provost waved the train off on its first-ever southward journey. Maguire and his mate, fireman Wilson, handed over to a replacement crew at Newcastle, travelling passenger on to York on a later service. They then lodged overnight before taking the down service back to Edinburgh the next day at 6.40pm with the same engine.

The two Coronation trains passed each other about two miles south of Darlington and both arrived punctually on that first day, as they were to do all week. The guard's journal gave the following passenger numbers for 5 July:

Down – on departure 64; alighted York 15, joined 7; on arrival 56.
Up – on departure 78; alighted Newcastle 11, joined 26; on arrival 93.

The fact that the late Mr Allen recorded the down service as being filled to capacity is puzzling in view of the figures given above. Possibly company employees made up the numbers, although one would not expect the guard to differentiate between fare-payers and complementaries in totalling seats filled, and it is significant that the numbers varied very little over the next few days and weeks in what was to become a disappointing record of custom. This is discussed in more detail later. Mr Allen's account was written up in his book *British Pacific Locomotives* in the 1960s, and he may have been confusing the 5 July journey with another of a different date.

The paucity of passengers may not have been obvious when the down Coronation arrived at Waverley, owing to the crowds waiting to see the first-ever train to connect London and Edinburgh in six hours – something

An unusual rear three-quarters view of the down Coronation about to plunge into the smoke of Ganwick tunnel with No 4490 *Empire of India*, Driver Coates at the regulator. The colour-light signal was not a common feature of the East Coast at this time, 12 August 1937, most of the signals being semaphores.
(*E. R. Wethersett/Millbrook House*)

Werrington troughs offer replenishment for one of the 'Commonwealth' A4s, No 4489 *Dominion of Canada*, on the down Silver Jubilee in the summer of 1939.
(*Gresley Society*)

which had not been done on a trial trip by the LNER and not attained even in the 1895 Race to the North when the timetables were torn up and the fastest time attained was still 20 minutes slower than that of the A4. According to newspaper accounts, the down train had to be eased from Dunbar as it was ahead of time, and the crew were being pressed to sign autographs for half an hour after arrival. Driver Hutchinson was quoted as saying, 'They're marvellous engines all right, and they ride nicely.'

The locomotives which featured on the Coronation's first day were actually working home. No 4491 *Commonwealth of Australia* was a Haymarket engine which must have worked up to London on the Saturday or Sunday after heading the Scottish press run on 2 July. It was to notch up 47 more runs out of the first 51 on the new streamlined train, running 23,000 miles with balancing turns included. Nor did age weary this fine engine – in the summer of 1957 No 60012, as renumbered, operated around 70 Elizabethan rosters on the non-stop schedule between London and Edinburgh – a record, and one achieved in the locomotive's twentieth year. What a pity the locomotive was not to be preserved by overseas admirers as was its counterpart on the up service. No 4489 *Dominion of Canada*, the A4 that had failed to go

above 109mph the previous Wednesday, nevertheless delivered its train on time at King's Cross.

Although the earliest A4s were fitted with corridor tenders, crews changed at York on the down Coronation and at Newcastle on the up. As soon as the engine had stopped, cleaners from the nearby sheds hurriedly climbed aboard the tender and shovelled coal forward to assist the new fireman – there was no steam-operated coal pusher as on the German 05 or the LMS Princess Coronation. The crews came from King's Cross, Gateshead, and Haymarket, in the same way that the Flying Scotsman was diagrammed, resulting in complicated and surely unnecessary lodging turns for the Newcastle men when the latter service was non-stop in summer. The fact that one depot from each of the three operating areas was involved in running both services was an indication of how devolved the LNER's management was. Even more importantly it gave all three areas an opportunity to participate in running the system's most important trains

– a boost for staff morale that had been missing from the Silver Jubilee operation.

Coal consumption was to prove a crucial, and quite unanticipated problem on the Coronation, and will be examined later in this chapter, under breakdowns. Water replenishment was not expected to provide problems as running non-stop between London and Newcastle and Edinburgh had been practised since 1927 in the case of the former destination, and since 1928 in the latter's. Six sets of troughs existed over the 393 miles between the two capital cities, five of them south of Newcastle. (See plan on p. 59.) It was anticipated that the final set of troughs on the down journey at Lucker, south of Berwick, might provide less than a full pick-up as the tender would have lightened so much, as coal was consumed, preventing the scoop from making a full insertion. In fact, examination of the guards' records suggests that up trains

Coronation luggage label, for use on Down services. (*WSS collection*)

had more trouble in scooping here, as taking water at Newcastle appears to have been more common on the southbound run.

* * *

The Coronation's seat reservations were not inconsiderable – 6s 0d (30p) or 4s 0d (20p), for the whole journey; probably one-tenth of present-day prices. They were, however, lower than corresponding supplementary fares for Pullman trains, for example 9s 0d (45p) for London–Edinburgh. In contrast, dinner, served at the passenger's seat, was 5s 0d (25p) First or 4s 6d (22½p) Third, surely a bargain, even after allowing for inflation! A pot of tea cost 6d (2½p).

As already observed, the observation car provided 16 duplicate seats, which could be booked by passengers for an hour at a time. LNER Staff Circular 298 was issued in June 1937 to explain the unique arrangements for these two vehicles. Tickets for the seats were issued on the train

only, by a 'lad attendant', one of three passengers' stewards on the train. Charging 1s 0d (5p) an hour, the young steward would sell (and immediately tear up) tickets on the following timetable (all times below are pm):

Period	Down journey	Up journey	Ticket colour
1st	4.15– 5.15	4.45– 5.45	Red
2nd	5.30– 6.30	5.55– 6.55	White
3rd	6.45– 7.45	7.05– 8.05	Light Blue
4th	7.50– 8.50	8.15– 9.15	Yellow
5th	9.00–10.00	9.25–10.25	Mauve

The later bookings could not have revealed much of the surrounding countryside in spring or autumn, particularly on the up journey. Not surprisingly, the car was dispensed with in autumn – from 4 November 1937 to 2 May 1938 and from 26 September 1938 to 3 July 1939, the latter comprising a fairly lengthy hiatus. They were also removed, for no obvious reason, between 15 and 26 June 1938.

In effect these unusual vehicles, so synonymous with the Coronation service, ran for only about 40 per cent of the train's career. Nor were the car end windows, with their curved perspex, as suitable for viewing passing scenery as they might perhaps have been; and so the cars had their ends re-designed in post-war years to improve the view when they were on later service in the West Highlands. Admittedly by then there was no question of their viewing ends being intended to improve air resistance at speed, but the whole necessity of having such coaches on the Coronation is economically questionable in view of their additional tare weight, negligible financial receipts (£4 maximum per journey) and a fairly limited view. 'Experience proved that not many passengers wished to leave their seats in the train' reports Newsome.

The only account this author has been able to trace of what Coronation passengers thought about travelling in these innovatory vehicles comes from Mr Ray Cox. His double 'streamliner' journey, already mentioned, included a southbound Coronation trip, mainly spent in the observation car. Surprisingly, so thick did he find the exhaust smoke that he had to abandon timing the train on Stoke bank by sighting the quarter-mileposts. He also found that the car '. . ."wagged" violently as we took Bridge junction (near Doncaster) at a very considerable speed', as he recalls. In the absence of glowing recollections from the nation's rail passengers about the joys of travelling in the LNER's observation cars, perhaps an open verdict on their appeal and operational

LONDON & NORTH EASTERN RAILWAY

DOMINION OF CANADA

EDINBURGH
WAVERLEY

THE CORONATION

effectiveness must be delivered. Had war not intervened it is possible that their future would have been reviewed by the LNER. Perhaps a cocktail bar should have been added to make them more attractive?

TABLE A
Sample of Coronation Passenger Use

Month	Week No	Average daily no of passengers			
		(dep)	(arr)	(dep)	(arr)
		Up		Down	
July 1937	1	101	106	71	53
Aug	5	108	124	122	79
Aug/Sept	9	127	162	132	90
Sept/Oct	13	119	155	131	81
Oct	17	90	131	100	57
Nov	21	79	119	92	54
Dec	25	85	67	137	86
Jan 1938	29	78	123	91	52
Feb	33	84	127	84	52

Newcastle stop inserted into Down timetable, 7 March 1938

Month	Week No	(dep)	(arr)	(dep)	(arr)
Mar 1938	37	108	144	131	56
April	41	93	147	177	96
May	45	79	117	134	69
June	49	115	159	173	96
July	53	118	153	164	99
Aug	57	100	127	182	97
Aug/Sept	61	133	162	175	105
Sept	65	119	151	189	130
Oct	69	108	142	153	80
Nov	73	91	126	134	74
Dec	77	91	120	188	102
Jan 1939	81	83	125	137	59
Feb	85	84	129	134	66
Mar	89	78	122	147	96
Apr	93	129	175	183	67
May	97	86	132	160	79
June	101	99	134	167	82
July	105	107	150	186	99
July/Aug	109	85	127	189	93
Aug	113	71	91	152	76

Average daily passenger complement (Up) = 98 on departure, 132 on arrival.
(Down) = 106 on departure, 67 on arrival.
(after Newcastle stop added) = 167 on departure, 86 on arrival.

Sample note: Average passenger patronage has been calculated from the statistics for every fourth week. 'Class distinctions' ignored. The reason for the difference in the number of passengers starting and completing the entire journey, was because of intermediate stops. It will be immediately noticeable from these figures that the Up train, which stopped at Newcastle from the outset of the service, conveyed more passengers to its final destination than the Down, with its stop at York only. A Newcastle stop was introduced in the northbound direction from 7 March 1938, but surprisingly, the York stop was retained, even though those joining the train there were few.

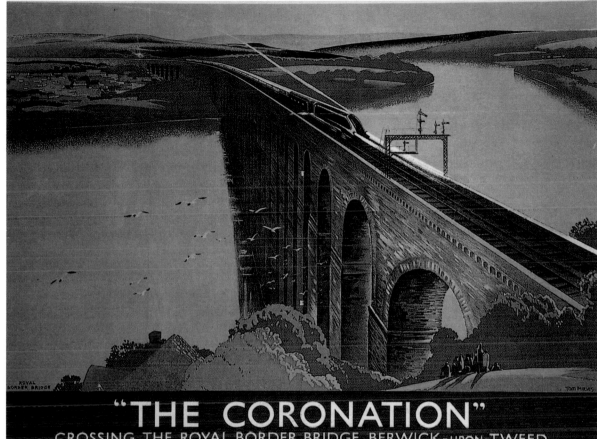

"THE CORONATION" CROSSING THE ROYAL BORDER BRIDGE BERWICK-UPON-TWEED. IT'S QUICKER BY RAIL. FULL INFORMATION FROM ANY L·N·E·R OFFICE OR AGENCY

LOADINGS, PUNCTUALITY, EFFICIENCY
Loadings

The LNER must have been terribly disappointed with the Coronation's patronage initially. Not even half of the 216 seats in the nine-coach rake were filled on an average day in the first fortnight; the down train loaded particularly lightly, with only around 53 passengers arriving at Edinburgh each evening (the numbers for the first five arrivals were 56, 55, 39, 51, and 64). Ironically, these numbers could just about have been accommodated in a Bugatti diesel railcar! The average loading for the down King's Cross–York leg was approximately one-third full, but after an average quota of 26 passengers had alighted at York, the remaining passengers from London were joined by no more than an average of seven more for the second half of the northward journey. (See Table A.)

The omission of a Newcastle stop in the down

How the LNER portrayed its only Anglo-Scottish streamliner, seen in this 1930s poster crossing the Royal Border Bridge over the Tweed. This delightful scene by artist Tom Purvis is slightly stylised in its detailing of the train, particularly its headlamps! A postcard of this scene is currently available from the National Railway Museum, York. *(National Railway Museum)*

direction, presumably done to prevent taking traffic from the simultaneous 4.00pm departure to Leeds and Newcastle and the Silver Jubilee following from King's Cross within 90 minutes, was obviously commercially damaging. Veteran railway expert R. E. Charlewood had predicted in a letter to the technical press in December 1936, eight months before the service began, that the new train would be a certain success 'provided there is an intermediate stop at Newcastle'. He was of course proved absolutely correct.

No 2512 *Silver Fox* whistles for the photographer as it heads the down Coronation near Claypole in 1937, the first year of the train's operation.   (*RAS Marketing*)

Sixteen lucky passengers were able to ride the Coronation's observation car for an hour at a time, on payment of 1/– (5p) per hour. The rear windows were perspex and the car's appearance was uncannily like that predicted by Norman Bel Geddes in his freelance design for an American streamlined train, published some time earlier.   (*RAS Marketing*)

After the inclusion of the Newcastle stop in March 1938 there was a healthy improvement in the passenger figures on departure from London, an average of 167 seats being occupied, as opposed to 106 before Tyneside travellers were catered for. On arrival at Waverley, the down service was still loaded disappointingly lightly, with little immediate improvement in seat occupation. (The reasons for the differing commercial prospects for stream-lined trains to and from Edinburgh, as opposed to Newcastle, are discussed in the Postscript.) The last sampled week's statistics before the Newcastle stop was added show a daily average of 52 passengers on the down Coronation arriving at Waverley; the first weekly sample after 7 March produced an average of 56. However, by the end of the train's life at the outbreak of war, the average daily arrival complement at Waverley stood at 86, compared to an overall average of 67 before the Newcastle stop was added.

In the up direction, the Coronation was leaving Waverley with an average of 101 passengers in its first week, thirteen of whom would alight at Newcastle, but an average of 37 joined on Tyneside, taking advantage of a fast train up at 6.33pm. This gave a London arrival only 55 minutes later than the 2.05pm up from Edinburgh, 4.29pm out of Newcastle. The first week's average passenger complement on arrival at King's Cross was 106, exactly double that of the northbound train on arrival.

It must have all been very disappointing for the company. No Coronation service ran at full capacity until the up train steamed into King's Cross punctually on Friday 3 September 1937, fully nine weeks after the service began. Fridays were invariably busier than any

Right: A4 No 4467 *Wild Swan* accelerates the down Coronation out of Gas Works tunnel on an unknown date in 1938.   (*RAS Marketing*)

A fine shot of No 4492 *Dominion of New Zealand* departing from King's Cross with the down Coronation on 19 April 1938. Interest in the train was obviously not just confined to 'spotters'. *(L. Hanson)*

other day, with Monday the second busiest, but even so, the up train had an average daily complement overall of only 132 on arrival in London, barely 62 per cent of capacity.

When one remembers that for 40 per cent of its operational life the Coronation was conveying an extra coach in the form of an observation car which effectively gave passengers a second seat on request, the over-capacity of the train becomes painfully apparent, particularly since the down service patronage had not improved much on the southern part of its journey, and was even more sparsely filled north of York. The historian is tempted to wonder if the LNER considered extending the Coronation on from Edinburgh to Glasgow (Queen Street). Glasgow was a conurbation at the time larger than either Birmingham or Tyneside and would have probably welcomed a train offering such a late afternoon departure from London (which the LMS Coronation Scot should really have provided) and fast connections to

and from North East England and Yorkshire.

Nonetheless, figures submitted to the LNER board on 14 September 1938 suggested that the gross revenue from the Coronation over a four week period to 9 July was £12,748, making the train the network's biggest streamlined earner. In the second volume of his book *A History of the LNER*, former company employee Dr Michael Bonavia reckons the net earnings after crewing and operational costs as £10,730 for the four weeks. Considering that the trains ran a total of 786 miles each day for 20 days during this period, the net revenue earned per mile works out at 68p compared to 65p for the

A4s Nos 2510 and 4500 under heavy repair at Doncaster. The latter appears to be carrying *Sir Ronald Matthews* nameplates, which dates the picture after March 1939 but before World War II, during which the A4s had their valances permanently removed. *(RAS Marketing)*

Jubilee. At least there is no evidence that the Coronation was taking traffic from other services – for the obvious reason that there was no other late afternoon departure from London and Edinburgh for the other destination – so this does at least appear to be pure profit, even if not an outstanding one.

Interestingly, there is evidence that demand for seats on the train occasionally outstripped capacity, and that harassed guards on the up service seated excess passengers in the observation car if a booking error caused the train to leave with more passengers than seats. On one such (surely rare) occasion, the guard's report has the pencilled words 'There were no complaints!' On another occasion, members of the Australian cricket team touring Britain in 1938 found themselves seated in Third instead of First, but again no fuss was made.

Punctuality

There have been heavier or faster British trains than the Coronation, there have been trains travelling longer distances non-stop, but never has there been a train travelling so fast, so far, so frequently, so reliably.

Not a single minute was lost on any of the ten journeys made in the first week on this exacting schedule – in comparison the LMS Coronation Scot was allowed an extra half-hour for a journey only eight miles longer. The Coronation dropped an average of 13½ minutes per week (against a weekly average of three minutes gained) in the first eight weeks, but that period included the height of the holiday season, with all the congestion that special workings could create, and the biggest single delay during this period was caused by a signalbox fire in Northumberland which cost a total of 41 minutes delay to both up and down trains out of a total of 109 lost. Only a handful of minutes were booked against the locomotives. In that

Hurrying through London's suburbs for Scotland, A4 No 4466 *Herring Gull* spreads its wings with the down Coronation around 1938. Six years later this locomotive was renamed *Sir Ralph Wedgwood* in honour of the chief general manager who had championed the idea of steam power for the LNER's streamlined expresses. *(RAS Marketing)*

'Neck and neck' A4 No 4467 *Wild Swan* and A3 No 4480 *Enterprise*, blast their way out of Gas Works tunnel on their way north from King's Cross, with respectively, the Coronation and the 4.00pm Leeds/Newcastle departure. The date is unknown, but precisely this side-by-side departure was arranged as a 'photo-call' by the LNER on 20 July 1937, six months before this A4 entered service.   (*RAS Marketing*)

first two months of operation, out of 76 journeys, 62 (approximately 81 per cent) were completed punctually or early, a magnificent achievement over a densely-used system at holiday time.

In comparison, in the final eight weeks, before the threat of war made Thursday 31 August 1939 the last day on which the LNER's streamlined trains ran, 58 out of 74 Coronation journeys were completed on time or early, again at the height of the holiday season. Indeed, nearly 50 minutes were gained on schedule – against which 144

minutes of lateness were recorded, an average of nine minutes lateness for each unpunctual service. This was despite the fact that down journeys then included a second stop, at Newcastle as well as York, effectively making the schedule some eight or nine minutes more difficult to keep than in 1937. Both two-month sample periods included a Bank Holiday weekend, when no Coronation services ran on the Friday and Monday. (See Table B opposite.)

TABLE B
Comparison of Punctuality: Coronation Service over First and Last 8 Weeks

	Total number of services	Punctual/Early		Late	
		No	%	No	%
First 8 weeks	76	62	81.5	14	18.5
Last 8 weeks	74	58	78.0	16	22.0

Note: The sample is drawn from July/August 1937 and 1939, obviously the height of the holiday season. The Coronation did not run at Bank Holiday weekends in either year, and the 1939 sample closed on the Thursday of the final week because of the imminence of war. It should be remembered that by 1939 the down service had a more difficult schedule than on introduction.

Table C exhibits punctuality data from a consecutive sample of one hundred Coronation services taken at random from a period outside the height of the holiday season, or the depths of winter.

TABLE C
Sample of Punctuality of 100 Coronation Services, 31 March–15 June 1939

	Up	Down	Total (mins)
On time	19	22	–
Early	21	15	64
Late	10	13	78
Total journeys	50	50	–

As can be inferred from Table C this sample of the Coronation's one hundred runs over a period between 31 March and 15 June 1939 (inclusive) produced 77 punctual or early arrivals, against 23 unpunctual. The up train had a slightly better record than the down as might be expected, with only one stop to make, as opposed to two for the northbound service.

The sample period included one failure on the road, No 4483 *Kingfisher* being replaced at Newcastle on the down journey on 7 June by A1 No 2571 *Sunstar*, and nearly a quarter of the cumulated total of 78 minutes lateness was taken up by this incident. Another A4 damaged its water scoop on a southbound journey and had to take water at Peterborough, but these two mishaps were the only occasions when time loss could be blamed on the engines or crews. For the rest of the sample journeys, the Coronation maintained its 77 per cent punctuality record despite sheep straying on to the line at Goswick, signal wires breaking in several places,

dynamo belts working loose on the coaching stock, and permanent way slacks springing up like mushrooms on every part of the line.

Confirming the above samples, suggesting a punctuality rate from 77 per cent to 80 per cent, comes a contemporary report from the technical press that the down train had been only 20 per cent unpunctual when passing through Newcastle during the period from July to November 1938. This included a complete month with not a single minute lost. It was a magnificent record for a high-speed service run by labour-intensive steam locomotives over a rail network far busier than today's and with more junctions and signals to set potential problems for the crews. Strangely, this record appears better than the Silver Jubilee's in the period 1935–37.

Of course, punctuality could only be maintained as far as weather conditions allowed. On 7 December 1938 both up and down services were early, to a total of four minutes, despite having to negotiate a total of seven permanent way slacks, but later that winter timekeeping became impossible. Heavy snow descended on the East Coast main line on 25 January 1939, delaying traffic, cutting visibility and causing signalling failures. A mishap on the former GNR section made necessary a diversion via the Hertford loop, adding to the chaos.

Another factor crucial to the success of the train's operation concerned the performance of the fireman. Some criticism had previously surfaced in the technical press about the effects of the LNER's 'big engine' policy – of running huge rakes of coaches on services where the passenger supply hardly justified such over-capacity – as this obviously added to the locomotive's work, and by implication to the fireman's. There was no question of the steam engine's firebox being fed by mechanical means, as was frequently the case abroad, on for example the Hiawatha and the Asia Express; manual labour was required, and as an added difficulty had to be done with the fireman's face towards the driver in order to allow easy communication between the two in a noisy environment. On a left-hand drive engine, as most LNER locomotives were by this time, this meant that firing had to be done with more strain being placed on the left wrist than on the right, not exactly favouring the dexterous.

Apparently Gresley ordered Eric Bannister to investigate the question of mechanical stoking for his Pacifics

The down Coronation at Helpston in August 1937, powered by No 4490 *Empire of India*, the locomotive which ran out of coal at Hitchin in the first winter of the train's operation. (E. Neve)

and the P2 2–8–2s, but the war intervened. Obviously the question of reducing the manual labour involved in fuelling Britain's streamlined locomotives was not given a high priority by management, demonstrating that humanitarian considerations did not loom large in managerial thinking. This also ignored the fact that the larger the locomotive firebox the greater the potential benefit might be in filling it mechanically and thus improving locomotive performance without any psychological constraint on the driver in wishing to spare his crew mate.

Firing techniques varied for different classes of locomotives, and for different duties. A long-distance non-stop journey required rates of firing unlike those on a stopping service, and when continuous high speed was required, the margin for error was increased accordingly. Coal had been consumed at 43 lb/mile by the unstreamlined *Papyrus* on its high-speed trial run in 1935, but this could be equalled or even exceeded if an A4 was fighting adverse side or head winds.

Obviously, the faster the train travelled, the more quickly each mile was covered, requiring fairly continuous firing action to maintain the rate of coal being fed to the firebox. Geoff Goslin calculated that on an up journey over a two-hour stretch from south of York to south of Stevenage the fuel requirement would require to be 3,350 lb/hr, 'more than ten per cent greater than that later defined by BR as the maximum sustained rate to be expected from a fireman'. This was 1½ tons of coal to be shovelled per hour, while also attending to injectors, taking water from troughs, and assisting the driver with signal sighting at particular locations. It seems incredible that no rail manager or crewman appeared to regard the installation of stoking equipment as necessary. Not only would this have been humane, it would have actually aided performance – a driver could put his locomotive flat out if need be, without worrying about the effects on his hard-working mate.

Breakdowns

The fastest British train over a distance greater than 300 miles, the Coronation, could hardly fail to pose an unprecedented challenge to locomotive endurance. Gresley Pacifics had been running non-stop between London and Edinburgh since 1928, a distance without equal in the world at that time as a daily achievement, but the Coronation was a different proposition entirely.

While the new streamlined express made one stop in each direction in this 393 mile sprint (two in the down

direction from March 1938), this was for three minutes only – insufficient to give the locomotive crew much time to use the blower on the fire, or to make anything but a cursory inspection of the reciprocating parts below footplate level. It was virtually a non-stop run in all but name, and scheduled for a higher average speed than the fractionally longer Coronation Scot of the LMS and at a far higher average speed (admittedly with a lighter load) than the then non-stop Flying Scotsman, which had only come down to a seven-hour schedule that summer. By the end of that year the Coronation's locomotives were breaking new ground by completing all 393 miles of the London–Edinburgh journey throughout the winter; through workings had never previously been attempted later than September.

Not long after the service's introduction, the *Railway Magazine* published logs of three up runs made in July and August 1937 by No 4491. All were accomplished punctually but the most eye-catching performance had been timed by O. S. Nock on 3 August and included 106mph down Stoke Bank at Essendine. The 12.7 miles from Little Bytham to Werrington junction had been averaged at 103.5mph, compared to 98.4mph by No 2512 on 27 August the previous year, or 92.4mph by No 4489 on the London press run on the previous 30 June. Cecil J. Allen had timed another '100' with No 4491 on the bank that summer. Given the LNER's lack of crew training, it comes as no great surprise to learn that the 106mph was attained by a driver making his first run on a streamlined train – Driver Walker of Gateshead may, like Driver Taylor in 1935, have been unaware of the high speed he was attaining.

This does not appear to have been the case on 3 August 1939 when a young Coronation passenger congratulated the driver at King's Cross after a southbound run when 107mph was attained down Stoke. Driver Nicholson promptly disagreed, claiming 110! The passenger was Mr R. A. J. Cox on the return leg of his reward trip on the Jubilee northwards and Coronation home again. 'The highlight of the run was the descent of Stoke Bank during which my inexperience with a stopwatch at very high speed and swirling smoke caused me to lose track at 107mph.' Mr Cox recalls that two teak coaches had been marshalled in the stock, and the resultant confusion over seat reservations at Newcastle caused a late departure, spurring the crew to run hard. Mr Cox's report of a five-minute early arrival at King's Cross (he estimates a 227 or 228 minutes net time) is confirmed by the official LNER

report on the run, although no mention is made of stock alterations.

The running of the Coronation had to be carried out by footplate staff and train crew while under constant scrutiny from senior management. Archival LNER files in the public records contain a daily summary of the Coronation's progress as collated at Liverpool Street and then circulated jointly by the superintendent and passenger manager of the LNER Southern Area to the divisional general managers in the Southern, North Eastern and Scottish Areas as well as to the chief general manager and chief mechanical engineer (Wedgwood and Gresley, no less). Every half minute lost had to be accounted for; any serious delay had to be the subject of a separate appended report.

It is almost impossible for the modern railway enthusiast to imagine what a routine journey was like on the Coronation. The logs published by those such as Cecil J. Allen recount unusual as opposed to routine performances, while the detailed LNER reports deal only with breakdowns. It could of course be argued that out-of-the-ordinary express running was required to keep the demanding schedule, particularly in the northbound direction.

What was an everyday, punctual journey like on this forgotten streamliner? We can be forgiven for posing the question, for the modern reader is not alone in uninformed speculation. One of the chief general manager's daily report sheets now in the public archives has a comment scribbled in pencil by an anonymous hand beside the passenger figures: 'Including me, I wanted to know what it was like!' Presumably this copy was not passed to Sir Ralph Wedgwood or Sir Nigel Gresley! The unknown railwayman who wrote this is not alone. Unfortunately, the record of breakdowns and emergency locomotive substitutions is not likely to tell you what a Coronation journey was like; indeed, with its tale of operational woe, it is almost unfairly unrepresentative, bearing in mind the 77 per cent punctuality rate.

Resplendent in shop grey with white lining – right down to the tender axleboxes – No 4489 *Woodcock*, soon to be renamed *Dominion of Canada*, stands at Doncaster. The A4 has been fitted with a converted A3 corridor tender whose coal capacity has been reduced to eight tons to allow the addition of the rounded fairing near the cab. The loss of a ton of coal soon proved to be a major handicap, before the year (1937) was out.
(*National Railway Museum*)

Nevertheless this historical source cannot be overlooked. So, while insisting that a history of out-of-course incidents does not represent the overall story of the Coronation, it is nevertheless worth examining, and analysing some of the breakdowns.

Table D lists 39 breakdowns on the Coronation while under way. Out of an estimated 1,084 runs, this works out as an apparent failure rate of about 3.5 per cent. Of these 39 'failures', four resulted in punctual or early arrivals, plus three only a minute late on arrival, giving effectively a failure rate of one in every 33 journeys.

Possibly this failure rate was inflated by the caution shown by locomotive crews in requesting a replacement engine if they so much as *suspected* that something was amiss or likely to develop as a problem. It is no coincidence that 31 of the 39 replacements (plus three requests for pilot assistance without the train engine being removed) took place at recognised locomotive centres where standby engines were always available. Of the eight failures in the 'middle of nowhere', two happened at Newark, where on at least one occasion a V2 was almost immediately available. The other substitutions occurred at Potters Bar, Abbots Ripton, Crow Park, Durham, Claypole, and Alnmouth, with such substitute motive power as a J6 0–6–0 and a G5 0–4–4T being commandeered to head Britain's fastest long-distance train.

With a tight schedule to be observed, a driver could not spare a few minutes to attempt to right a mechanical problem himself, as he might on a lesser train, but requested the replacement immediately. In three of the 39 cases of replacement, the 'invalid' locomotive was running Britain's fastest long-distance train on or ahead of time! In other words, the Coronation's so-called failure rate is artificially distorted by the train's very importance, and the crews' determination to pre-empt mechanical failure.

As if to underline the arduousness of the task, and the possibly over-careful attitude it generated among footplate staff, notice that the first year's service of the Coronation produced 21 breakdowns on route, as compared to one in the first twelve months of the Silver Jubilee. Against this, must be pointed out the fact that the Silver Jubilee frequently involved a double working for the A4 concerned – 536 miles daily as opposed to 393.

An unusual case of a crew attempting to carry out its own running repair happened early in the Coronation's career, on 22 October 1937. No 4489 *Dominion of Canada* lost some 13½ minutes on the early part of the journey on the down service due to a missing valve cap. At Grantham, although a pilot engine was waiting to take over, the A4's driver borrowed a cap from the replacement and fitted it himself. The train was 15 minutes down on schedule by York, but the northern part of the run was always an easier proposition than the southern, especially before the addition of the Newcastle stop six months later, and Edinburgh was reached only five minutes late, suggesting an excellent time of some 187 minutes for the 204 miles from York to Edinburgh start-to-stop. However, this kind of running repair at the crew's own initiative was exceptional, and was seldom repeated in the Coronation's later history; indeed it may have been officially discouraged when replacement engines were so freely available.

Table D offers as complete a record as possible of locomotive replacements on the Coronation. It omits an occasion on 29 October 1937 when the up train was diverted via Lincoln and the locomotive had to be replaced as its tender was too high for the water crane at Doncaster. This hardly constitutes a 'failure' as the train was already substantially late because of the diversion. Also omitted is an incident on 25 August 1937 when the down train reached Waverley station but had to be assisted the last few yards into the platforms, making its arrival 13 minutes late. Possibly the A4 lost its grip in the Calton tunnel following a signal check.

The Coronation's first breakdown in 'the middle of nowhere', away from a recognised locomotive centre, was also its most serious. On Tuesday 16 November 1937, the up train, headed by No 4488 *Union of South Africa*, failed completely north of Potters Bar at about 10.25pm. According to the special report which management demanded on this stoppage, the locomotive's 'big-end brasses had gone' but the Pacific could neither move nor be moved, suggesting that the brakes had seized. A replacement engine and fitter were immediately sent for from Hatfield, but after some 20 minutes' work, Driver Hirst of Gateshead informed the local station master that his engine was now in a fit state to be removed from the train. N2 0–6–2 tank No 2666 was immediately appropriated from a down local and drew the entire assembly to the Potters Bar up home signal, enabling the wounded Pacific to be sidelined. N1 No 4582 had by now appeared from Hatfield (presumably working light on the wrong line with all the holdups *that* would cause) and had the honour of hauling the crack express down the hill to King's Cross, arriving 83 minutes late. At least five following up trains were delayed by the incident, two of them arriving more than 70 minutes late – No 4488 had been inconsiderate enough to fail on a two-track section. Despite this blemish, this Haymarket Pacific went on to a distinguished career, hauling the last up Coronation before the War, and the first up non-stop Flying Scotsman after, as well as the last up steam-hauled non-stop express between the capitals in 1961. In addition, as we shall see, No 4488 may have achieved the fastest-ever northbound journey on the East Coast main line. This locomotive is now preserved.

The onset of winter produced more examples of operational problems for the LNER authorities. On 2 December the up Coronation was again in trouble on the former GNR section; this time No 4490 *Empire of India* created something akin to history by running out of coal at Hitchin. Its tender was designed to hold eight tons, normally allowing a 20 per cent reserve on the usual six to seven tons consumed by Gresley Pacifics on the nonstop London–Edinburgh services since 1928. But the latter were *summer* services, and No 4490's failure – surely unprecedented on East Coast main line services – was to cause the LNER authorities a rethink on the A4's tender design.

But that was a long-term process; Hitchin shed was able to offer a C1 Atlantic No 3272 as a pilot on this occasion, the delay lasting 16 minutes. Presumably the A4 was not totally incapacitated and was able to assist in at least getting the express under way again, although speed would necessarily be restricted on this section, as doubleheading was not allowed at speed on Welwyn Viaduct. King's Cross was reached 19 minutes late.

According to the RCTS history of LNER locomotives, A4 No 4492 also failed at exactly the same location on an up Coronation one week later to the day. C1 4–4–2 No 4427 was attached on this second occasion, but the incident was not mentioned in the official report sheets sent to the chief general manager. Nor was the reason for failure recorded; presumably it was another coal shortage. Certainly, crews on the northern section of the express's run were reportedly finding coal rations meagre as the Scottish capital was neared each evening, although there seems to have been no record of a complete failure from this cause on a down service.

Nevertheless, the matter had to be given attention. From the introduction of the A4s, as already pointed out, the new Pacifics were constructed with corridor tenders

TABLE D Locomotive Replacements on Coronation Express

Notes: E = early ** = not traced

Date	Direction	Failed A4	Replacement Class and No	From	To	Arrival min late	Comment
1937							
16.9	Up	4491	A3 2597	Newcastle	King's Cross	1	Time gain
24.9	Down	4490	A1 2577	York	Waverley	12	
4.10	Up	4489	A1 2568	York	King's Cross	59	Lost 23
16.11	Up	4488	N1 4582	Potters Bar	King's Cross	83	
13.12	Up	4489	A3 2505	Newcastle	King's Cross	5	
14.12	Up	4490	A3 2597	Newcastle	King's Cross	24	Also fog
30.12	Down	4497	**	Newcastle	Waverley	9	
1938							
10.1	Up	4486	A3 2505	Newcastle	King's Cross	28	4486 assisted by C7 2165 Tweedmouth–Newcastle
19.1	Up	4490	A3 2507	Newcastle	King's Cross	11	4490 on time
21.1	Up	4496	A1 2546	Grantham	King's Cross	17	Also fog
28.1	Down	4488	**	York	Waverley	12	
8.3	Down	2512	A3 2746	Newcastle	Waverley	10	2512 1 min early
9.3	Down	4497	V2 4782	York	Newcastle		
			A3 2503	Newcastle	Waverley	1 E	
10.3	Down	4488	A1 2577	York	Newcastle		
			A1 2575	Newcastle	Waverley	13	
13.5	Down	4488	A3 2507	Newcastle	Waverley	11	
17.5	Down	2512	A1 4473	Grantham	Waverley	55	
13.6	Down	4488	**	Newark	York		
		**	A1 2575	York	Waverley	41	Time again
17.6	Down	4482	A1 2570	York	Tweedmouth		
		**	**	Tweedmouth	Waverley	45	
21.6	Down	4467	K3 2428	Hitchin	Grantham		
			A3 2744	Grantham	Waverley	38	Time again
23.6	Up	4497	A3 2598	Newcastle	King's Cross	1½	Time gain
23.6	Down	4485	A4 4490	Newcastle	Waverley	1	Time gain
24.6	Down	**	**	Newcastle	Waverley	On time	Time gain
7.7	Down	2510	A1 2571	Newcastle	Waverley	6	
20.7	Up	4487	V2 4773	Newark	King's Cross	29	
24.10	Down	4487	A3 2746	Newcastle	Waverley	48	Time gain
9.12	Down	4483	C1 4413	Abbots Ripton	York		
			A1 2577	York	Waverley	61	
20.12	Up	4487	A3 4480	Crow Park	King's Cross	48	
1939							
4.1	Down	4482	W1 10000	Grantham	Durham		
			G5 1837	Durham	Newcastle		
			A1 2575	Newcastle	Waverley	57	
9.1	Down	4486	A3 2746	Newcastle	Waverley	6	
12.1	Up	4467	J6 3580	Claypole	Grantham		
			A1 2546	Grantham	King's Cross	71	
13.1	Down	4464	A4 2511	Newcastle	Waverley	On time	Time gain
2.2	Up	4485	A1 2476	Grantham	King's Cross	15	
13.3	Up	4902	A3 2747	Doncaster	King's Cross	5	Time gain
22.3	Up	4491	A3 2595	Newcastle	King's Cross	On time	Time gain
24.3	Up	4493	C7 2205	Tweedmouth	Newcastle		
			A3 2507	Newcastle	King's Cross	23	
7.6	Down	4483	A1 2571	Newcastle	Waverley	18	
16.6	Down	4497	V2 4782	York	Newcastle		3 min early at York
			**	Newcastle	Waverley	17	
1.8	Down	4496	A1 2571	Newcastle	Waverley	1	1 min early at Newcastle
21.8	Up	4465	A1 2582	Alnmouth	Newcastle		
			A4 4499	Newcastle	King's Cross	32	

Some information on locomotive identification has been added from tables compiled by Leslie Burley and published in *The Gresley Observer*, Nos 95 to 99. The author acknowledges this useful source of information with thanks; all the other data above is taken from archival file BR/LNE/8/359 (SRO).

Responsible for the fastest-known steam-powered run between King's Cross and Edinburgh was No 4488 *Union of South Africa*. Seen here when brand new on 22 June 1937, this Pacific overcame an eight-minute late departure from King's Cross in August 1939 to reach Waverley punctually in 352 minutes actual, including two stops, giving a possible net time of 340 minutes. The locomotive is now preserved as BR No 60009. (*National Railway Museum*)

with coal consumption limited to eight tons owing to the space taken up at the front of the coal bunker by a metal fairing designed to continue the engine's 'streamlines' back from the cab. This was all very well, but the fact was that a ton of coal had to be sacrificed, compared to the 1928 design of corridor tender prepared for the introduction of non-stop services between London and Edinburgh in that year. These vehicles had managed to include a corridor through the right-hand side of the tender to permit crew-changing on the move, while at the same time *increasing* the then standard eight ton coal capacity to nine tons, as recounted in this author's book *Non-Stop!*. Interestingly, the completion of the first corridor tender

was executed at Doncaster within 50 working days of the drawings being received – an accomplished piece of pioneering construction which certainly finds a parallel in the brisk no-nonsense way that the LNER's streamlined coaching stock was conceived seven years later.

So strong was the 'streamline' craze, that it was decided around 1936 to similarly treat all these earlier corridor tenders, even if it meant sacrificing a ton of coal, considered not to be a potential problem on a 268 mile run such as that of the lightweight Silver Jubilee. The short-sightedness of this policy was first seen at Hitchin when longer journeys began to be undertaken all the year round. Running an express, streamlined or not, into a persistent headwind, inevitably meant a rise in coal consumption, and the fairings on the A4 tenders were removed over the next three months, during the 1937–38 winter. Some of the earlier 1928 tenders, which had been streamlined for their transfer to A4s, now had to undergo a second modification in a very short time.

Another modification which took place late in 1937 was caused by a fatal accident on the Coronation. On 8

October Inspector Skinner, riding in the cab of the southbound train, was hit by a wall of water thrown up as the two Coronation trains took water simultaneously at Wiske Moor water troughs, between York and Darlington. The water from the northbound train overflowed from the A4's tender, hitting the up train's engine at a combined speed of around 140mph, shattering the cab window and causing fatal injuries to the inspector. Modifications were immediately put in hand on the tenders to reduce the likelihood of such overflows recurring, while the cab windows were replaced with armour plate glass.

Fortunately, this fatality was to be an isolated, indeed unique, incident in the story of the Coronation, although the problems continued as the first winter set in. On 10 December, the very next day after the second December substitution at Hitchin, an unidentified A4 had to take on a pilot engine (also unidentified) at Peterborough on the up train. 'Shortage of steam' was the reason recorded, 9½ minutes being lost in attaching the assisting engine, while more time was dropped because of a permanent way slack at Abbots Ripton and the compulsory slowing at Welwyn, making the King's Cross arrival fourteen minutes late.

Three days later, in what was rapidly proving to be the Coronation's worst month up to that time, No 4489 had to be removed from the up train at Newcastle for an unspecified reason. The train had been three minutes late through Berwick, but was only four minutes late away from Newcastle with No 2505 *Cameronian*, one of the last batch of A3s, in charge. One minute was recovered before Doncaster, but three permanent way slowings made a punctual arrival impossible, and the Coronation reached London five minutes late.

*   *   *

Failures on the Coronation continued into 1938 as the LNER's engines and footplate crews wrestled with the problem of running high-performance trains during a severe winter. The second week of March produced two failures on the down train in successive days, the second of which saw a very fine performance from a substitute engine.

On Tuesday 8 March No 2512 *Silver Fox* was heading the down Coronation, its silver-grey livery at some variance with the two-tone blue of the coaching-stock. Newcastle was reached one minute early (this was only the second day of a stop being scheduled here), but the engine was classed as having failed, for no recorded reason, and Gateshead A3 No 2746 *Fairway* substituted. The lateness away from Newcastle is not known, but seven minutes were subsequently lost to permanent way checks and Edinburgh reached ten minutes late.

Remarkably, the very next day was to see another, very similar, problem occur on the down service, but with a more spectacular result. No 4497 *Golden Plover* was taken off the express at York, being replaced by V2 No 4782, the usual three minute stop being doubled by this substitution. Nevertheless, despite this three-minute late start, Newcastle was reached one minute early!

According to the RCTS history, the V2 was here replaced by A3 No 2503 *Firdaussi*, which passed on to Scottish territory one minute early, despite meeting slacks at Acklington and Beltonford, and the northern destination was reached also one minute to the good. Incredibly the official (guard's) report on the train's journey, while confirming the replacement of the A4 at York and the early arrival at Edinburgh, does not mention

the second substitution at Newcastle. This is a strange omission from an official report intended for the eyes of the chief general manager and chief mechanical engineer, and throws absolutely no light on what must have been a creditable episode of railway operation. If the Newcastle changeover was achieved in only three minutes, this was commendable indeed. More probably, one minute was lost here, arrival behind the V2 being one minute early, and the time gained to Marshall Meadows, where Scottish Area metals were reached just after Berwick-on-Tweed, was at least three minutes by a non-streamlined engine on a 66½ minute schedule for the 67 miles, slacks included.

The engine replaced in the above incident, *Golden Plover*, was credited with running for two months on the train with a break only for a public holiday, accumulating a mileage during those eight weeks of nearly 19,000 miles including balancing Saturday mileage, with a large proportion of it at an average of more than 70mph. It achieved 84 per cent punctuality during 25 recorded arrivals at Newcastle on the more difficult down service during this period, and on one occasion was no less than five minutes early.

In May 1938 No 2512 *Silver Fox* was again a culprit,

failing on the down train at Grantham on the 17th. Nine minutes were lost here while it was replaced by A1 No 4473 *Solario*, and the Edinburgh arrival was no fewer than 55 minutes to the bad. Ten minutes had been lost by the locomotive being forced to take water at Berwick, suggesting a failure to pick up at Lucker water troughs. In a recent book entitled *Non-Stop!*, the history of long-distance express operations across the Anglo-Scottish border, this author mentioned an occasion when an A1 Pacific ran all the way from Edinburgh to London on the Coronation with a single load of coal in an eight ton capacity GNR tender. That occurred on the very next day, 18 May, which is significant in that it had originally been thought necessary to increase the Pacifics' coal supply from eight to nine tons to allow a reasonable

A stand-in hero on the Coronation in June 1938 was unstreamlined A3 No 2744 *Grand Parade* which gained ten minutes on schedule from Newark northwards, including what is believed to be the second-highest speed ever recorded by steam on the East Coast main line north of Newcastle. The A3 is seen here heading the 4.00pm ex-King's Cross at New Southgate – this train continued to run at the same time after the Coronation's introduction, the two sometimes leaving side by side. (*RAS Marketing*)

reserve for long journeys, a provision which had been regarded as unnecessary when the first A4s emerged. Yet here was an A1 with its original tender being (very surprisingly) turned out by Haymarket to work the up Coronation.

It was a remarkable decision by the depot, an almost unique rostering of a non-streamlined engine to the most demanding of the expresses designed for the exclusive haulage of A4s, made at a time when Haymarket already had no fewer than ten A4s of its own, plus a number of A3s more modern than *Solario*. Presumably, the Haymarket shed staff, who took to Edinburgh-born Gresley's engines from the moment they first crossed the Border, felt that nothing was beyond a Gresley Pacific! In fact, *Solario*'s King's Cross arrival on the Coronation was six minutes late, with water being taken at Newcastle, but with three permanent way slacks encountered.

On 21 June 1938 an eventful northbound journey was

Gresley's 'Hush-Hush' 4–6–4 No 10000 was rebuilt with a conventional boiler and A4-type streamlining in 1937. When called on to head the down Coronation at short notice in January 1939, the engine failed after about 150 miles, although it did haul a later Silver Jubilee punctually. (*RAS Marketing*)

completed 38 minutes late at Edinburgh after No 4467 failed no farther north than Hitchin. K3 No 2428 ran the train forward over Stoke summit to Grantham, covering 74 miles in a highly creditable 76 minutes start to stop, including a permanent way slack. A3 No 2744 *Grand Parade* then took over, its performance including a 120 minute dash from Newcastle to Edinburgh *including* the station stop. O. S. Nock reported in 1945 that this particular run had involved a time gain of no fewer than ten minutes between Newark and Waverley, including 99mph north of Newcastle, believed to be the second highest speed recorded on this section. (He cited a 100mph sprint between Belford and Beal by No 4486 *Merlin* on another Coronation journey as the fastest.)

1939 was only four days old when the northbound Coronation experienced trouble at Grantham. No 4482 *Golden Eagle* had to be removed (no reason recorded) and was replaced by No 10000 the 'Hush-Hush' 4–6–4 whose appearance had so impressed Norman Bel Geddes. This locomotive's outline had now changed, an A4-like streamlined casing replacing the earlier profile. Ten minutes were lost here, but worse was to come, the substitute developing a hot bearing on one of its driving-wheels. It had to be ignominiously removed at Durham,

so Sunderland-based G5 0–4–4T No 1837 had the honour of hauling the Coronation the nine miles to Newcastle. Here A1 No 2575 *Galopin* was waiting to take over, so the train's fourth engine brought it into Edinburgh 57 minutes late. Incidentally, No 10000 redeemed itself by heading a Silver Jubilee punctually later in the year.

At this time, Gateshead allocated an A1 or A3 to shadow both up and down Coronation services. The standby engine moved into Newcastle (Central) at 6.15pm, waited until the up train was safely off southward, and was then turned, presumably over the King Edward Junction and High Level bridges, before taking up position to provide cover for the northbound train at 8.00pm. On 23 June 1938 one replacement engine proved to be insufficient, as both up and down services failed on Tyneside! Nos 4497 (up) and 4485 (down) had to be removed from their trains with the same complaint, a broken little end pipe. A3 No 2598 *Blenheim* set off for London with a will, reaching King's Cross only 1½ minutes late, despite encountering two slacks, while A4 No 4490 *Empire of India* was available for the down service, covering the Marshall Meadows to Edinburgh stretch in only 51 minutes, and reaching Waverley barely one minute late – a commendable double performance.

Meanwhile, on 11 January 1939, the first A4 to be based on Tyneside, No 2511 *Silver King*, showed its class on the down Coronation by taking over at Newcastle from No 4464 and reaching Edinburgh on time, covering the Marshall Meadows–Waverley stretch in 50½ minutes. Twelve days later, No 4490 *Empire of India* achieved a complete northbound journey on the Coronation in 363 minutes, despite losing eleven minutes to permanent way workings, suggesting a very fast net timing during the depths of winter.

On 2 February 1939 No 4485 *Kestrel* (renamed *Miles Beevor* in 1947), which had been two minutes ahead of schedule at Shaftholme, succumbed to a damaged brick arch in its firebox and came off the up train at Grantham. Its replacement was one of Gresley's original A1s, a great favourite on the former GNR main line, No 4176 *Royal Lancer*. Unfortunately, there was to be no spectacular time recovery by the older Pacific; 13½ minutes had been lost at Grantham, and this probably does not take into account braking and accelerating time on either side of the stoppage. Not too surprisingly, King's Cross was reached 15 minutes late, but it is conceivable that the veteran picked up a few minutes on this exacting schedule. *Kestrel* redeemed itself at the end of the month by

A4 No 4485 *Kestrel* proved to be both a villain and hero on the Coronation service in February 1939. After failing on an up train at Grantham, having to be replaced by A1 No 4476 *Royal Lancer* the A4 made a fine run northwards later in the month, recovering seven minutes north of York on a delayed service. *Kestrel* is pictured here at Dundee in 1938. (*W. E. Boyd Collection*)

reaching Waverley only one minute late after leaving London one minute down, an arrears which had increased to seven minutes by York because of a delay at Potters Bar followed by no fewer than five permanent way restrictions. The 124.5 miles between Newcastle and Edinburgh were reeled off in a half minute less than two hours, including standing time at Central station – a typically unheralded run of considerable accomplishment.

March 1939 was a chequered month in the Coronation's history, producing a number of remarkable runs from substitute engines. On the 13th of the month, double-chimney A4 No 4902 *Seagull* ran hot and had to come off the up service at Doncaster. The replacement was A3 No 2747 *Coronach*, but there was nothing 'funereal' about progress southwards! According to the frustratingly sparse details in the LNER record sheets, there was a ten-minute stop at Doncaster for this substitution, but London was reached at 10.35pm, only five minutes late. If one assumes that the Doncaster delay was 16 minutes net (ten standing, three each for time lost to braking and then accelerating), the time gained was eleven minutes on a 73mph schedule over 160 miles (Shaftholme–King's Cross).

It is a pity that we do not know the precise timings involved, as this A3's performance was surely not far away from a 77mph average between Doncaster and London. Unhappily, *Coronach*'s performance seems not to have been recorded in the railway press. This much under-rated locomotive was soon to be (rather wastefully perhaps) re-allocated to Carlisle Canal depot, working regularly over the Waverley route, where 60mph was a rare occurrence.

One of the fastest journeys southbound on the Coronation may have been made by A3 No 2747 *Coronach*, substituting for a failed A4 at Doncaster, averaging not far off 77mph on to King's Cross. The locomotive is seen here with an experimental cutaway smokebox door (1931–33) intended to clear smoke from the driver's view – something the A4's wedge-shaped front did so satisfactorily. (*RAS Marketing*)

Two Gateshead A3s made historic runs southwards when taking over the Coronation in emergencies twice in the same week in March 1939. On the first occasion, No 2595 *Trigo* reached the capital in 229 minutes (a gain of eight minutes on schedule). This was possibly the second fastest southbound run by steam on the East Coast main line south of the Tyne. Here *Trigo* is seen leaving Newcastle on an up train in 1932.   (*RAS Marketing*)

The older A3s continued to show that they could rival their streamlined sisters in performance. Before the month was up, on 22 March, No 2595 *Trigo* substituted at Newcastle to replace No 4491 and reached King's Cross punctually in 229 minutes. Confirmation of the guard's times would be welcome, but there was obviously a time gain made, and this may have been excelled only by a run two days later, and by the same crew. With A3 No 2507 *Singapore* replacing a C7 Atlantic which had made an emergency substitution at Tweedmouth, the 268 miles from Tyneside to London were accomplished in 227 minutes (including three permanent way checks), very probably a record for steam in the up direction. Driver Nash and Fireman Gilbey of King's Cross were the men responsible for both these outstanding runs.

The official LNER record sheet dealing with the record run on 24 March does not confirm the locomotive and crew details, which have passed into history. What it does record is a departure from Newcastle 34 minutes late, with no fewer than eight minutes being lost at Central. This was caused by not only changing the A3 for the C7, but by a bizarre accident. So keen was fireman Gilbey to get the Coronation under way again that he forgot to couple the engine to the train!

According to the record submitted later by the guard, the delay was increased by the renewal of 'heater pipe broken by fireman omitting to couple up engine'. In the circumstances, the loss of only eight minutes here was commendable indeed, in view of the repair required, and the figures in the LNER file speak for themselves – left Newcastle 7.07pm, arrived King's Cross 23 minutes late at 10.53pm. Shaftholme was passed in 93 minutes for the 108 miles start to pass, the remaining 160.2 miles being accomplished in 133 minutes. This source gives the Newcastle–London time as 226 as opposed to 227 minutes actual – whichever is correct, it was a record for steam power. How ironic that it should be accomplished by an unstreamlined Pacific.

The late Eric Neve, railway historian, has suggested that a supplier's error in the labelling of drums of lubricating oil may have been responsible for the sequence of failures during this particular month, but there was at least the consolation of some record-breaking runs in the resulting emergencies.

April 1939 saw a fine performance on the down train on the 11th, when a three-minute early arrival was achieved at Edinburgh, despite the Pacific concerned, No 4489, leaving London one minute late and encountering three permanent way checks. The Coronation's last summer was a good one, as the random sample quoted

Bettering *Trigo*'s effort by almost three minutes was a dash on the up Coronation with the same crew on No 2507 *Singapore*, here seen in its final form in May 1964 when fitted with a double chimney and German-style smoke deflectors. This A3's 1939 record was all the more remarkable for the fact that, so anxious to restart the delayed streamliner were the footplate crew, they forgot to couple the engine to the train, breaking the steam heating pipe when the Pacific pulled out for London on its own! *(Mitchell Library)*

Although a Tyneside-based locomotive for all of its working life, A4 No 4465 *Guillemot*, seen here at Haymarket, had the unusual distinction of being the last A4 to fail on the Coronation, having to be taken off the up train at Alnmouth some ten days before the service ceased for ever. *(RAS Marketing)*

that the record of arrival times at stations was regarded as unsatisfactory, and the entries for the northbound run of 25 August 1939 are consistent throughout its record progress. No 4488, now happily preserved as No 60009, had produced the final flourish on the most operationally challenging streamlined service of them all.

Six days later, on Thursday 31 August 1939, the final up train pulled into King's Cross behind No 4488 one minute late (due to adverse signals), 32 minutes after the corresponding down service had reached Edinburgh one minute early, hauled for the last time by No 4487. The one minute leeway in each direction neatly cancelled out. The Coronation was a resounding success of steam-powered rail operation, achieving a better punctuality record than the Silver Jubilee, and on a much tougher timing than the rival Coronation Scot – albeit at a higher expense of locomotive failure.

Britain's railways were never to see its like again.

THE WEST RIDING LIMITED

Leeds and Bradford were connected with the capital by streamlined train from 27 September 1937. On the face of it, this seems a remarkably late appearance for such a service, given the potential for catering for return business journeys between London and these important industrial centres on a daily basis, and not least because this was the test track for the high-speed run by *Flying Scotsman* in 1934. It appears that the viaduct over the River Calder near Wakefield was the problem, preventing Pacific operation before 1930, and thereafter only with a stiff speed restriction until 1936, when the structure was renewed sufficiently to allow A4s to cross, although not at full speed. On the steeply graded section between Leeds and Bradford, motive power was provided by a brace of N2 0–6–2Ts. Reversal was carried out at Leeds (Central), with coupling and uncoupling taking place simultaneously at each end of the train.

Two A4s were publicly allocated to the service, with names specially appropriate to the world of textiles – No 4495 *Golden Fleece* (after running for a fortnight with the name *Great Snipe*) and No 4496 *Golden Shuttle*. Both were allocated to King's Cross, none of the class ever being allocated to a Leeds depot.

Like the motive power, the footplate crews were provided by King's Cross depot. Six crews (drivers Beach, Giddens, Long, Nash, Ovenden, and Rayment) were organised into a new 1A Link for the operation of the new train, despite the remarkable fact that none reportedly

earlier shows, with only 10½ minutes booked against the locomotives (apart from the one run featuring a replacement) out of a total of 600 scheduled running hours. On 15 August the up train had the temerity to be six minutes early at Hitchin, and was promptly punished by a six-minute signal stop at Knebworth and a two-minute late arrival at King's Cross. It was not unknown for the up train to catch up with the 2.05pm out of Waverley if the latter were running badly, as happened at Stevenage on 21 December 1938.

Six days before the cessation of the service, an intriguing entry appears in the official records – a down service left King's Cross eight minutes late owing to a points failure following an electrical storm, all but one minute of the arrears being recovered by Newcastle, and the Edinburgh arrival being achieved punctually. The official log gives the following timings, with this author's estimated net times added:

	Schedule (mins)	Actual	Estimated Net
York *arr*	157	152	–
Newcastle *arr*	237	230	224
Edinburgh *arr*	360	352	340

The actual times of 230 minutes to Newcastle and 352 minutes to Edinburgh with two stops, surely constitute a record for steam, the net times being probably around 225 minutes to Newcastle and 340 to Edinburgh, assuming that station standing times were cut. From information added by a Gresley Society member, we know that the locomotive concerned was No 4488 *Union of South Africa*, the victim of the train's first breakdown, here redeeming itself with a brilliant run. Driver Ferguson of Gateshead is understood to have driven No 4488 on one stretch of the run, the other driver not being known at the time of writing.

While rail historians are loath to accept guards' journals as records of outstanding times, it should be remembered that these logs, now preserved in the public archives, were intended for scrutiny by senior, indeed top, management. Some discrepancies in the recorded passing times in July 1939 were the subject of official investigation, but the documents contain no indication

Its bell is highly prominent in this August 1939 shot of No 4489 *Dominion of Canada* as it heads south from Darlington on an unidentified express. (*RAS Marketing*)

had any experience of high-speed running. Even more remarkably, the LNER ignored the established expertise of the Pullman Link at Leeds Copley Hill depot, where, according to local enthusiast Michael Joyce, Messrs Berridge, Bird, Malthouse, and Rogers had 'hoped that they might, at least, have been given an opportunity to share the working of this prestigious new train'.

Like the stock for the Coronation, that for Yorkshire's own streamlined service, the West Riding Limited, was ordered from Doncaster in October 1936. Consisting of four twins identical to the Coronation, the stock carried the same external livery, although different interior decoration was applied. No observation car was included

Up from Yorkshire comes the West Riding Limited behind one of its 'own' A4s, No 4496 *Golden Shuttle* around 1938. This locomotive is now preserved in the USA as BR 60008, with its post-war name *Dwight D. Eisenhower*. (*RAS Marketing*)

11.30am nears at Leeds Central station as No 4496 *Golden Shuttle* waits for the West Riding Limited to complete the first part of its journey from Bradford, before taking it on to London. The corridor tender, not strictly necessary for any streamlined express, can be seen to advantage. (*National Railway Museum*)

Porters (on left) sprint towards the West Riding Limited at platform 5 at King's Cross on 16 June 1938 as blue-liveried *Silver Link* brings the train to a halt. Records show that this arrival was punctual and that No 2509 worked both up and down services for four successive days that week. (*National Railway Museum*)

because of the reversal at Leeds. As with the winter formation of the Coronation, that of the Limited amounted to 278 tons tare, accommodating 48 First and 168 Third class passengers. Supplements of 4s 0d (20p) and 2s 0d (12½p) were charged for each class respectively.

The train began its day at Bradford (Exchange) at 11.10am, re-starting from nearby Leeds (Central) at 11.31am after a three-minute stop, and reaching King's Cross at 2.15pm. Going down, departure was unusually late at 7.10pm, arriving at Leeds at 9.53pm and Bradford at 10.15pm. Overall, the average speed was 63.3mph in both directions, with the main part of the journey between London and Leeds scheduled for slightly below 68mph (up) and slightly above 68mph (down). Between Leeds and Doncaster the average speed was 51mph, a quite creditable timing considering the steep climb (1 in 50 at one stage) out of Leeds and the speed restrictions over the South Yorkshire coalfield.

Criticism has been made of the very late departure time from King's Cross, causing the express to mesh with evening fitted freights heading north, while timekeeping between Doncaster and Leeds was apparently affected by any delays to the previous down Leeds service, the 5.50pm out of King's Cross, due into Central only ten minutes before the new train. The obvious solution to the problem would have been to start the 'Limited' at 5.50pm or just before the 'omnibus' Newcastle express, with the slower train following later. The up service could have been retimed for up to an hour earlier to continue offering something like four hours in the capital.

Despite its comparatively slow progress north of Doncaster, there should be no doubt about the quality of running required to keep the West Riding Limited's timetable. The 163 minutes (down) and 161 (up) were not bettered until the 1960s, and included an 85mph timing over the 27 miles between Hitchin and Huntingdon and 72.7mph over Stoke bank northwards.

Like the other two streamlined trains, a press run was planned for the new streamliner, this being designed to woo the Yorkshire media and community leaders. No 4495 headed the eight-coach set from Bradford and Leeds to Barkston and back on Thursday 23 September 1937. The 75.2 miles from Leeds to this triangular junction four miles north of Grantham was achieved in 77 minutes. The train reversed at Barkston and returned to Yorkshire, the maximum attained being 94.5mph on the outward journey near Crow Park. Alderman Tom Coombs, Lord Mayor of Leeds, was pictured in the locomotive cab at Barkston, and the resulting press attitude showed that the trip had been well worthwhile. One newspaper referred to the train as a 'rhapsody in blue'; how often do present-day British railway initiatives receive this kind of reception? Public service began the following Monday, although not without incident.

The roster for the new train involved the King's Cross engine working down to Yorkshire the previous Sunday on the 6.10pm King's Cross–Leeds. It was programmed to work up on the first streamliner from Leeds, at 11.31am the next morning. Unfortunately, when No 4495 was sent north on the Sunday evening – it had reached London after hauling the previous Thursday's press train – it ran hot at Doncaster. No 4492 was hurriedly sent north at 1.30am on the morning of the first West Riding Limited and brought the train up to London, as well as the next two down and up services. No 4492 had just completed 62 journeys on the non-stop Flying Scotsman roster – a pre-war record.

Driven by Driver Beach of King's Cross, No 4492 reached London two minutes early with Yorkshire's long-awaited streamliner. The first down journey, crewed that evening by Driver Long and Fireman Allfrey, was less fortunate. Despite a fine run to the outskirts of Doncaster in 126 minutes 44 seconds at an average of 71.6mph, including a signal stop lasting nearly two minutes, the train was held up by the 5.50pm so badly from that point northwards that arrival at Leeds was 14¼ minutes late. The next day's up journey was 3¾ minutes early, with '100s' being attained at Crow Park, as well as in the usual location down Stoke bank.

The service appears to have received less attention from rail enthusiasts than the other LNER streamliners, possibly because of the difficulties of timekeeping caused by traffic on the northbound journey. In 1938 double-chimney A4 No 4901 Capercaillie averaged 90.4mph on the Limited between Huntingdon and Hitchin, but the same year saw the only reported failure en route: No 4489 had to come off at Carcroft to be replaced by K3 2–6 0 No 1166. If this was in effect the only such failure, then it represents a magnificent operational record out of 968 journeys – 0.1 per cent. The two 'textile' A4s operated 55 per cent of the workings between them, although at least three Gresley A1s, including the one which started all this high-speed work, Flying Scotsman, were rostered to the service, as was V2 2–6–2 No 4789. On the last named occasion, 14 January 1938, the heavy mixed-traffic engine lost only four minutes on schedule.

Like its better-known contemporaries, the West Riding Limited ceased running as Hitler's war loomed large over Europe. On Thursday 31 August 1939, No 4495 brought the train into King's Cross and its counterpart No 4496 headed the last working of all back to the West Riding, on the line where Flying Scotsman had first proved it could be done.

THE EAST ANGLIAN

'The East Anglian will allow the business man of Norwich to devote two hours or so in the morning to current office duties, or his women folk to prepare for a West-End shopping expedition or matinee, before departing from Norwich at 11.55.'

In this way the East Anglian express was introduced to the readers of the LNER Magazine. (Obviously middle-class women were not expected to work in those days!) From 27 September 1937 Norwich and Ipswich were to enjoy a streamlined steam-hauled express service, much in the same way as considerably larger cities such as Newcastle, Glasgow, Edinburgh, Leeds and Bradford. Just how streamlined the train actually was is debatable, nor was the timetable a major advance on existing services offering greater accommodation, at least not on the London–Ipswich section of the run. What is undeniable was the luxury of the service offered, and the efforts of the railway staff to make it a success.

Six coaches were built at York for the service, conventional in appearance and without the kind of streamline features of the other three trains. The rake comprised Brake Third, First Restaurant car, First, Third, Third Restaurant car, Brake Third. At 61½ft each was longer than the Jubilee coaches and were centre-gangwayed like the excursion coaches of the time. Interior decor was stone and green for First class; buff and dark green for Third. Light fittings and parcel racks were chromium-plated. Fifty-four First and 144 Third class seats were available in a tare weight of 219 tons. The Railway Magazine said of this stock that it was 'neither articulated nor streamlined . . . and is of the company's standard construction'. No supplements were charged.

The East Anglian is seen in this fine shot near Ipswich on its run from Norwich to London (Liverpool Street), headed by B17/5 4–6–0 No 2859 East Anglian. (RAS Marketing)

Locomotive provision for the train was not the usual A4, as these were not allowed to operate on the former Great Eastern main line because of weight problems. The most important existing services were handled by the B17 4–6–0s, another Gresley locomotive, although not apparently designed by him.

The resemblance of the streamlined B17/5 4–6–0 No 2859 *East Anglian*, to the A4 class above footplate level is superficial, the streamline casing being obviously shorter and more squat, with the steam pipes showing above the cylinders. Note the blackout cover between cab and tender, fitted in anticipation of war conditions. *(RAS Marketing)*

Unusually for the LNER under Gresley's tenure of the post of chief mechanical engineer, the design of the B17 4–6–0s had been contracted out to a locomotive manufacturer. The North British Locomotive Company of Glasgow had already constructed twenty A1 Pacifics for the company in 1924–5, but this order for ten 4–6–0s for the former Great Eastern lines also included the design work, as Doncaster, busy with new designs and construction, was having difficulties in producing an engine powerful enough to replace the B12s, but with a light axle-loading. NBL apparently had equal problems and the first of the class were delivered late. Seventy-three were eventually built, twenty-one by NBL and Robert

Although unloved by many railway historians, no one could accuse Gresley's design of streamline casing of failing to lift exhaust smoke and steam out of the driver's view, as this pre-war picture demonstrates. B17/5 No 2870 *City of London* is seen on Halifax Junction water troughs near Ipswich on an ordinary Great Eastern line express. *(RAS Marketing)*

Stephenson, the rest at Darlington, but it was Nos 2859/70 that had a part to play in the streamline story.

The B17s had been first introduced in 1928, so the decision to streamline two of their number to operate the East Anglian between London (Liverpool Street) and Norwich was a somewhat surprising one. If anything, it

tended to underline suspicions that the train was being streamlined in name only – the coaching stock was conservative in outline, the locomotives from a class nearly ten years old. Obviously the need for the locomotives to have a light axle-loading was a crucial one as far as the former Great Eastern lines were concerned, prompting the decision to encase two existing locomotives in a shell similar to the A4s. It can be viewed by the transport historian as, alternatively, the extension of a successful design of streamline casing to other locomotives on the system, or of the debasing of an idea that was successful as a unitary concept of locomotive and train designed to transport passengers at high speed.

In September 1937 Nos 2859, a Darlington-built engine of 1936, and 2870 from the Robert Stephenson batch, and only four months old, emerged from Doncaster works in streamlined casings. To the untrained eye, the engines, newly designated B17/5, looked indistinguishable at a distance from an A4, apart from the lack of a trailing axle, although there were of course detailed differences – for example, the steam pipe above the cylinders was visible above the valancing. Some 3½ tons were added to the engine weight by the casing and by the side sheets of the tender being built up to emphasise the impression of streamlining. Livery was LNER green with the valances painted black, as was the 'prow' of the locomotive, the black being rounded off at the front as seen in profile.

The East Anglian service began on 27 September 1937, the same day as the West Riding Limited. The up train left Norwich (Thorpe) station at 11.55am each weekday, reaching Liverpool Street at 2.10pm after an intermediate four-minute stop at Ipswich only. The down train left London at 6.40pm, again stopping only at Ipswich. By February 1938 there was a slight rearrangement in the schedule, with the Ipswich stop being halved and three minutes cut from running times. The up train was then started at twelve noon.

There seems to be a consensus among railway writers that the East Anglian's schedule was not too demanding from an operating point of view, allowing 50 minutes (reduced to 48 in March 1938) for the 46.3 miles from Norwich to Ipswich and 80 for the 68.7 miles thence to Liverpool Street. The overall average speed required was 51mph, although mile-a-minute timings between these points were frequently achieved; an 80mph ceiling on the line may have made time-recovery more difficult in the

case of a delayed train. Water was picked up en route at Halifax junction troughs, allowing the Ipswich stop to be halved from February 1938.

The first day's running seems to have set the scene for what was to follow. Coming up to London, Driver Fryer and Fireman Wright of Norwich had No 2859 up to 80mph between Kelvedon and Witham and down Brentwood bank, with Liverpool Street being reached one minute early. In the opposite direction No 2870, crewed by Messrs Mace (driver) and Underhill, achieved 80mph before Colchester and reached Ipswich one minute early, and Norwich two minutes to the good.

'Timekeeping, as might be expected, was a simple matter.' So opined Cecil J. Allen in publishing his first reports of the new express. One of the earliest runs recorded in detail found No 2859 coming up from Ipswich fifteen seconds within timetable, achieving a maximum of 82½mph at Harold Wood. On the same day No 2870 went down to Ipswich in 78¼ minutes, both drivers treating speed restrictions with excessive caution. Allen made the point that the 9.48am out of Liverpool Street was allowed only two minutes more to Ipswich, despite regularly loading to 13 bogies, more than twice the load of the East Anglian. He believed that the train's schedule gave the crew some 14 minutes' leeway to recover from checks, and that the down service was easier to operate than the up.

One locomotive could handle both trains, although it was common for both these Norwich-based locomotives to follow a more complicated diagram involving them each in one daily working of the train. According to the RCTS history of the B17 class, one of the two streamlined B17/5s would work up to London on the East Anglian, leaving Liverpool Street only 90 minutes later on the 3.40pm down as far as Ipswich. Here the engine came off and worked the 5.15pm local back to Norwich, this usually comprising a few coaches. The second engine came up to the capital on the 2.15pm ex-Norwich and went back on the down East Anglian. When the rosters were modified to give the first engine more standing time in London, it returned on the 5.16pm back to Norwich, allowing both streamlined 4–6–0s to be seen in or around Liverpool Street at the same time.

The two engines operated these rosters on an alternately weekly basis – No 2870 running up 90,000 miles after streamlining by 27 March 1939 – while the coaching stock spent barely four hours out of every 24 in revenue-

earning service. Towards the end of 1938, No 2859 entered works for an overhaul and seems to have rarely featured on the working until the following April. With No 2870 following to be overhauled in March 1939, there was a lengthy period when the train was in the charge of non-streamlined engines, particularly No 2840 *Somerleyton Hall* and 2872 *West Ham United*, the latter regarded as Norwich's best.

One diversion which resulted in quiet country lines seeing their most opulent train took place on 26 January 1939. The up East Anglian was diverted by floods at Stowmarket via Beccles and the East Suffolk line, being the last train to get through. No 2870 was the train engine and it took the return working back to Norwich via Cambridge and Ely.

In April 1939 No 2859 was fitted with air raid covers over its cab to the tender front – a momentous omen. Sure enough, within five months World War II brought all British streamliners to a halt after Thursday 31 August. The East Anglian alone was to run again.

In 1941, just as the larger A4s were having their valances removed to facilitate maintenance, so did *East Anglian* and *City of London*. However, unlike most of the streamlined Pacifics, the two B17/5s were put into store at the outbreak of war, when all streamlined services ceased. Both engines were stored within three days of war breaking out, remaining unavailable for traffic until the following mid-February, an extraordinary state of affairs at a time when the LNER system needed all the power it could muster – indeed, it was later to import King Arthur class 4–6–0s from the Southern.

The East Anglian, unlike its more glamorous sister trains, managed to re-appear after the war, commencing on 7 October 1946 with the same rolling stock. The newer B1 4–6–0s were given responsibility for the train, which was frequently made up of eight coaches and run on a less demanding schedule, but it was not until the introduction of BR Standard Britannia Pacifics in 1951 that the two now-demoted streamlined engines had their casings removed, being re-designated B17/6.

There was an element of tokenism about the so-called streamlining of the East Anglian – not as fast as it might have been, without properly streamlined vehicles, but sharing the same luxury furbishment and leisurely under-employment in a four-hour day. One wonders if it was all a camouflage to disguise the LNER's less than generous service to East Anglia.

7 BRITAIN'S RAILWAYS AFTER THE STREAMLINE AGE

It is significant that the first two streamlined trains to operate outside North America – the German diesel *Fliegende Hamburger* and the steam-operated Asia Express – were each a product of a rigidly divided society where only a few citizens could expect to be whirled along to their vital destinations in mile-a-minute luxury. Perhaps it is not too surprising that the concept of an exclusive streamlined express did not catch on to the same extent after World War II, a war brought on by the nations which pioneered this symbol of social inequality, of discrimination, and of the exploitation of one human being by another. At least in the USA the concept of the streamlined express was used as an inducement for ordinary citizens to ride trains as opposed to aircraft, then still new and sensational. In Britain, on the LNER at least, the streamlined express was seen as appealing primarily to business travellers, creaming off such traffic from existing services.

World War II put an end to the story of British steam-powered streamlined express operations, although that was not immediately obvious in the austere times immediately post-war. A publicity booklet published by the LNER in 1946, called *Forward: the LNER Development Programme*, promised 'restoration of pre-war standards of service' as well as 'progressive improvements', and carried the following declaration in a kind of blank verse:

'Our famous streamlined trains
Silver Jubilee, Coronation, West Riding Limited
will require track in first-class condition
for their high speeds . . .
. . . their re-introduction must wait awhile.
But they will return just as soon as possible and,
no doubt, be more popular than ever.'

In fact, these streamlined expresses were never again to delight railway enthusiasts by running in their entirety in the post-war years. Their locomotives, the A4s, were to continue their tradition of high-quality performance for up to another 20 years, as will be documented in this chapter. However, the coaching stock was to have a less illustrious history after the war; indeed, the fate of some of Britain's finest railway coaches intended for public use, was one of disappointing and unimaginative under-utilisation.

All British streamlined stock was stored during the war, although four LNER vehicles came to a fiery end not long afterwards. Two Third class saloons and two Open Firsts were destroyed in a fire while working in the 3.45pm King's Cross–Leeds (Central) on 14 July 1951. A later Ministry of Transport inquiry found that a red-hot coal had fallen through a gap in the firebars of the train engine, A3 No 60058 *Blair Athol*, and was thrown up by a wheel through a gap in the coach floor of one of the leading ex-streamliner vehicles, where some asbestos lining was missing, but where sponge rubber was located for sound-deadening.

The resulting fire was undoubtedly made worse by the guard wrongly assuming that the smoke visible was coming from a hot box, so valuable time was lost while the official wrote a note to throw from the train instead of applying his brake. Indeed, passengers' lives were endangered, mainly because of the reduced number of doors and communication cords. When the train finally stopped in section at Huntingdon, some windows had to be broken to allow passengers to escape; twenty-two had to be treated for burns, nine being detained in hospital. The unfortunate guard was particularly badly burned as he tried belatedly to deal with the spreading conflagration.

While it could be argued that the concept of 1930s streamlined express trains seemed to have ignored safety provisions in the interest of comfort (minimising on draughty doors, using sponge rubber to deaden noise),

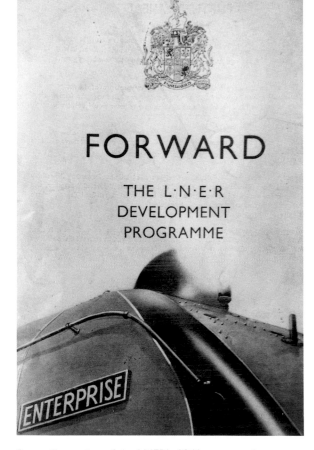

Cover illustration of the LNER's 1946 propaganda brochure, promising improved services when the company had fully recovered from the effects of war, and not ruling out the re-start of streamlined services. No A4 was ever called *Enterprise* – this was photographic licence to emphasise a point! (*WSS collection*)

the fact was that the coaches in the 1951 incident (ironically on the West Riding express) were full with standing passengers, something that was never anticipated when planned as part of an exclusive service.

The remaining stock from the Coronation had their undercarriage fairings removed and additional doors cut into their body sides. No attempt was made to employ the Coronation stock as a rake for a particular train, although two twin Firsts were used in the up and down Talisman expresses, but only from 1956. Ironically, axlebox roller bearings were fitted in 1957, when these coaches were 20 years old.

As already noted, the observation cars (originally numbered 1719 and 1729) were transferred to the Scottish Region, where they plied on the Glasgow (Queen Street)–Fort William–Mallaig line from 1956. In 1959 their rear sections were remodelled at Cowlairs Works with larger plate glass windows fitted and new armchairs installed, one of the two vehicles even receiving an internal tartan lining. They were withdrawn at the end of the 1967 summer season, after 30 years of somewhat patchy service – a good idea which never quite found its time.

Some of the stock from the earlier streamliner also found its way north of the Border. Five vehicles from the Silver Jubilee – a twin First and a triplet Third set – were allocated to the new BR Scottish Region in 1948. For no apparent reason, they found themselves gracing the otherwise obscure Fife Coast Express connecting Glasgow (Queen Street) with such East Neuk villages as Pittenweem and Crail. This was a summer working, the corresponding winter train running between Glasgow and Leven. On the face of it, this was an extraordinary use

The sloping smokebox front gives evidence of the previously streamlined state of No 46224 _Princess Alexandra_, photographed leaving Lancaster with an up express in August 1952, eight years after de-streamlining. (_RAS Marketing_)

of prestige stock. The restaurant car triplet was deployed more conventionally from 1948 on the 8.15am New-castle–King's Cross and evening return working. Why all eight vehicles could not have been used on the traffic for which they were intended, complemented by additional stock as required, is not immediately clear. Perhaps the newly nationalised management did not want to divert attention away from its new Tees-Tyne Pullman taking over the Jubilee's former departure timings, although there was surely enough custom for both trains. All eight vehicles were withdrawn by 1963.

The stock built for the West Riding Limited fared better after the war than the other LNER streamlined vehicles. Six coaches from the original rake were the first passenger vehicles to be painted in the BR 'plum and spilt milk' livery after nationalisation and formed the core of the new West Riding service. At least a constructive attempt had been made to use this specialised stock as a recognisable entity.

David Jenkinson first encountered this streamlined stock in the guise of the post-war West Riding. His reaction to it is particularly interesting and indicative that, even in utilitarian use, Gresley's streamlined stock was still very impressive:

'I can still recall my utter and complete astonishment when I walked into one of the open thirds. The first impression was that I was in the first class bit of the train, so I walked through to find the "steerage" part. When I finally did arrive at the genuinely first class portion, I realised to my delight that I really was not dreaming and that what I had taken to be first class was indeed third; for the firsts were quite unbelievable.'

As for the East Anglian stock, its non-streamlined nature would obviously lend itself more easily to every-day use, and so it proved. As already mentioned, the East Anglian service was re-introduced from 7 October 1946. The six original vehicles were, not surprisingly, supple-mented by two Thirds, while from 1951 one of the restaurant cars was dispensed with.

Over on the LMS, there was a similar dilemma being faced as to how best to employ streamlined stock. To use it all on everyday services seems to imply an acceptance that the brief golden years of high-speed train travel were over for the foreseeable future. Stanier's Pacifics – being

built in their unstreamlined form as late as 1947 – were losing the streamlined casings carried by 24 of their number. On 29 May 1946, the company's chief operating manager issued the following internal memo:

'It will be some considerable time before we shall be in a position on the LMS to contemplate the introduction of such high speeds as existed pre-war because of the effect of the war-time years on the maintenance of our rolling stock and track.'

Thirty-two vehicles now had to be found utilitarian employment, but since two-thirds of them lacked stream-lined attributes, whose absence was so disappointing at the time of their introduction, this certainly could be expected to ease their introduction into general revenue-earning service. Strangely, most of the stock appeared to have found a use working on super-commuter trains between Manchester and Southport, and Liverpool and Blackpool. Individual vehicles found their way into almost indiscriminate usage elsewhere on

Lacking its speed lines and with only the cabside clean, revealing the BR number, this former LMS streamlined Pacific had an imposing if unattractive appearance. No 46243 *City of Lancaster* was photographed at Crewe on 18 May 1948 running with LMS still showing through the grime on its tender. *(D. P. Rowland)*

the system, but the newer Third class coaches, seating as few as 36 passengers, did not, having little capacity to offer hard-pressed railway managers.

By its very nature, streamlined stock was unsuited to the everyday bustle of railway operating, not least be-cause of the articulated underframes and limited capacity. (The first Coronation Scot was an exception to the first point.) For these reasons it seems reasonable in retro-spect to question why such stock was not kept together in existing rakes for use on long-distance expresses, supplemented as required by additional Third class ac-commodation. The pre-war use of the Coronation Scot set on the Saturday Midday Scot and return Sunday working, while disappointing at the time in dissipating the streamlined train's exclusive aura, was an intelligent use of otherwise non-earning stock. Following the war, this should have been exactly the use to which the streamlined stock was put on both main lines north from Euston and King's Cross. Long-distance travellers were entitled to all the comfort they could get, after what they had been through in six years of war.

This sheer waste of high-quality stock is highlighted when compared with, for example, the LMS's record of coach renewals in the years 1940–4 – a mere sixteen vehicles per year (BTC figures quoted by Gourvish – see Bibliography). This for a company owning 22,000 passenger vehicles!

* * *

One is tempted to wonder if the LNER's 'development programme', referred to above, was nothing more than a propaganda exercise designed to neutralise any demand for railway nationalisation. LNER directors appear

Silver Link when ex-works on 21 August 1947. Resplendent in garter blue, minus nameplates, and bearing the new number 14, the pioneer A4 was photographed at Doncaster. (*D. P. Rowland*)

to have been in the van of those opposing nationalisation, although in view of Labour's huge majority at the time, and that party's obvious mandate for a programme of badly needed social and economic reform, such resistance was never likely to succeed.

Perhaps such speculation about the directors' sincerity is to do the LNER an injustice; it certainly appears that there was some consideration given by the company to the restoration of high-speed services as soon as possible. On 21 and 22 May 1946 an officers' high-speed special was arranged to run from King's Cross to Edinburgh and back, comprising six bogies of 205 tons tare, to be hauled by A4 No 2512 *Silver Fox*.

According to staff notices circulated beforehand, there was no doubt that an attempt was being made to simulate streamlined conditions after seven years; local area staffs were told that the trains (reporting numbers 361 down and 439 up) 'will run at speeds similar to those of the Coronation', although post-war speed restrictions on certain areas of track made impracticable a six-hour schedule, and the special was timed for 399 minutes down and 401 up.

Signalmen were instructed to treat the train with a special 'Is line clear?' telegraph message of '4 beats, pause, 4 beats' to communicate its passage and it was to be 'dealt with in accordance with the special instructions issued to all signal boxes and level crossing keepers concerned in connection with the working of the Coronation train'. Point-to-point times were similar to those of the pre-war streamliner, even down to the ambitious 72.6mph average between Dunbar and Drem in the down direction, but approaches to, and accelerations from, stopping places were noticeably slower.

On the two days of the trial, no difficulty seems to have been encountered in keeping time – indeed, the up journey seems to have been spectacular by the standards of the day, accomplished in 378½ minutes. There was a very fast 68 minute passage of the 80 miles between Newcastle and York, with 102mph later being attained near Essendine by Driver Kitchener. North of Newcastle, where the scheduling was only four minutes (down) and three-and-a-half minutes (up) outside the Coronation's timing, the Haymarket driver, Bell, contented himself with simply keeping time, with a maximum of 78mph on the northbound trip, during which the speedometer drive failed at Berwick. Stopwatch times were substituted without the trial being affected.

Why did this not presage a re-introduction of the fast expresses that the LNER had operated so well before the war? Official papers circulated afterwards specified 'the opportunity that the trials afforded of studying the present conditions of the track'. The permanent way's condition was obviously crucial and probably not of a standard high enough to permit high-speed running to the pre-war level; indeed, Britain's railways had a two-year backlog of permanent way maintenance by the end of the war, with repairs for the years 1940–4 running at 70 per cent of peace-time levels. It would not have been beyond the bounds of reason to re-introduce the streamliners on slightly relaxed timings, with an overall speed limit. After all, with the Flying Scotsman taking all of eight hours or more on the London–Edinburgh run, a seven or 6¾ hour Coronation re-introduction could hardly be anything but attractive to the travelling public. However, the time was probably not right, with nationalisation on the horizon, for such a bold step.

During that very summer of 1946, the operating staff of the LNER were preoccupied with a series of dynamometer tests on the Flying Scotsman. The 470 ton formation was to have the test car added on down journeys on 3 and 5 June, and up on 4 and 6 June. These

are not immediately relevant here, except that they confirm the heavy and slow nature of passenger expresses in the 1940s, and the conclusions drawn from the tests included recommendations that the Anglo-Scottish schedules be ironed out to make all sections equally accommodating to timekeeping.

Quite a flurry of paperwork resulted from these four tested journeys, the Scottish area in particular believing that summer conditions were the worst possible time to appraise timekeeping anomalies, and protesting that up journeys were not being officially recognised as being more difficult than down – which was certainly true of the

line north of Newcastle, including Cockburnspath, although this was arguably the opposite on the London–Newcastle stretch.

Incidentally, Cecil J. Allen seems to imply in his book *British Pacific Locomotives* that there was some possibility that the locomotive chosen for the May tests was an A4 in preference to A1 No 4470 *Great Northern*, the controversial Thompson rebuild of Gresley's first Pacific, although it is difficult to see why an unstreamlined engine should be even fleetingly considered for such a high-speed task. In view of No 4470's subsequent history, it is not at all surprising that it was passed over at operational

A4s at Paddington. As discussed in the accompanying text, the 1948 Exchange Trials seemed to lack any underlying rationale. In this shot, the chime whistle of No 60033 *Seagull* echoes around Paddington as it approaches with a test train, complete with dynamometer car.
(*RAS Marketing*)

level in favour of an A4, although it is possible that Allen had in mind the Flying Scotsman test rather than the quasi-Coronation one. One of the papers relating to the former refers to the opportunity of testing the new A1s 'of which there will be at least one in service in the Southern Area'. For the six-coach London–Edinburgh special, on the other hand, *Silver Fox* was officially specified in Circular AD40/1946 four days before the trial took place. Of course, all this simply confirms Mr Allen's contention that when a high speed challenge arose it was a Gresley A4 that was sent for, and not one of its new-fangled successors!

If the A4 had been intended to represent a departure from the LNER's 'over-capacity' policy of running trains of heavy tare weight irrespective of the traffic carried (of which more anon), the A4s soon found themselves taking

No 22 (later 60022) *Mallard* leaves Paddington with a Plymouth express on 26 April 1948 during the Exchange Trials. On the following day *Mallard* ran hot and had to be replaced by *Seagull*.   (*RAS Marketing*)

their place among their unstreamlined sisters, as well as new Pacifics from Gresley's successors, Thompson and Peppercorn, in operating heavy trains to less than demanding schedules. Fortunately, emergency workings during the war had shown an unexpected side to the A4's character – the ability to haul exceptionally heavy loads at nearly normal express speeds. Such feats recorded included the doyen of the class, *Silver Link*, taking 25 coaches – 850 tons gross weight – from London to Grantham in three minutes over two hours, while No 4901 *Capercaillie* ran 22 coaches (730 tons gross) at an average of nearly 76mph over a 25 mile stretch north of York. Not bad for a class designed to haul 250 ton trains at about 70mph!

In the first year of British Railways a programme of locomotive exchange trials was carried out. With the former LMS streamliners losing their casings at this time – the last was removed in 1949 – the A4s were the only class of locomotives left (ignoring the two B17/5s and the isolated W1) capable of operating streamlined trains in Britain should the new management decide on their re-introduction. But the 1948 exchange trials gave no hint of such a possibility; indeed, from the conduct of the exchanges it was difficult to gauge quite what the authorities' purpose was in organising such a programme.

The 1948 exchanges seemed to have been dreamed up with train spotters in mind; why trouble to test an A4 on the banks of Devon, or a Royal Scot on the Great

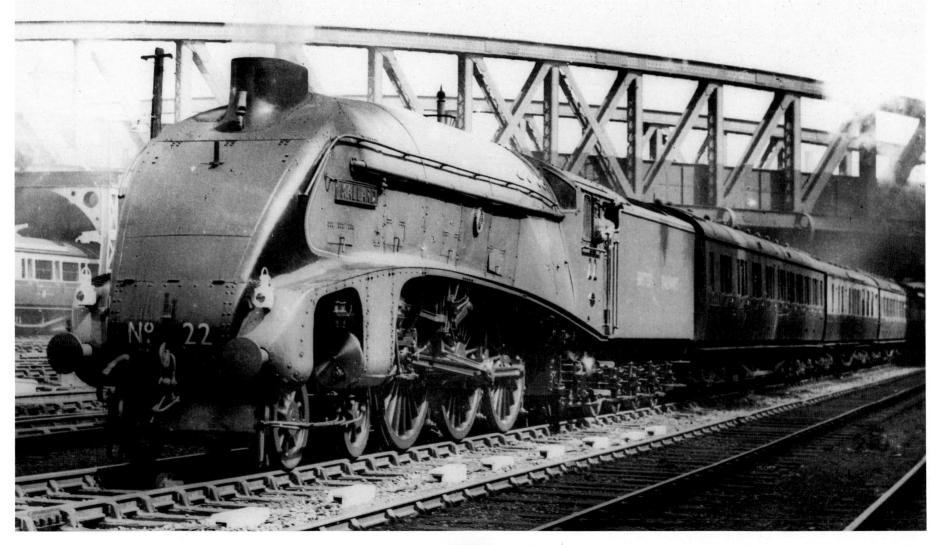

Northern main line when the indigenous motive power seemed to be coping perfectly well? Some tests, such as that of a Bulleid light Pacific over the Highland main line or in East Anglia were certainly well worth pursuing – and characteristically, were not – but the A4s, built for their special role of hauling lightweight expresses, were not tested particularly imaginatively.

In fact, no light Anglo-Scottish expresses aimed at business clientele, apart from Pullmans, were re-introduced on to East Coast metals until the arrival of the Talisman late in 1956. This eight-coach service offered, like the Coronation (and including two coaches from that

service) a late afternoon departure time from both London and Edinburgh, reaching the other city in 6 hours 40 minutes, with one stop at Newcastle. Streamlined A4s were prominent on the new service, and with good reason. With their valve settings improved by new optical techniques imported from Swindon, the Pacifics were embarked on an Indian summer of sustained high performance as a matter of routine.

The gradual (in fact, *too* gradual) introduction of double-chimney apparatus to the A3s and A4s was another factor in the longevity of both classes. Those four A4s which had enjoyed such a fitting when new, Nos

A4 No 60033 *Seagull* headed for the West Country from a second London terminus, in this case Waterloo, by powering the down Atlantic Coast Express on 10 June 1948. The former GWR dynamometer car is prominent in this picture.   (*RAS Marketing*)

4468, 4901–3, had shown some indication at the time of potentially improved performance over their single-chimney sisters, although it may have been worsening fuel and labour conditions during and after the war which emphasised the need for such an improvement. With the lapsing of the Kylchap patents during the war (according

A late 1950s shot of A4 No 60015 *Quicksilver* pulling out of Darlington with the northbound Fair Maid express, a short-lived extension of the Talisman express, its northern destination being Perth.   (*RAS Marketing*)

to P. N. Townend), it became very economical to fit both classes of Gresley Pacific with double-chimneys in their entirety.

It is arguable that this would have been economic even if patent royalties had had to be paid, since tests at King's Cross suggested a coal saving of up to 7 lb/mile on the double-chimney engines. That the remainder of the class were not converted until diesels were already entering service on the East Coast is surprising to say the least, the last two converted being *Gannet* and *Union of South Africa* in November 1958. Incidentally, when the A3s were fitted with double chimneys, drifting exhaust became such a problem for their crews that German style 'elephants' ears' deflectors had to be adopted to rectify the problem. So well designed were the A4s' wedge-shaped front ends that drifting smoke and steam was never a problem with the double chimney fitted.

*   *   *

If there was one job on Britain's nationalised railways which probably could not be done by any other locomotive class, it was the 'non stop'. This was the summer-only non-stopping service between London (King's Cross) and Edinburgh (Waverley) known as the Flying Scotsman in 1928–39, and again in 1948, then the Capitals Limited in 1949–52, and finally the Elizabethan from 1953 to 1961 (these years inclusive). The Elizabethan's final year was in fact 1962 when it ran on a six hour timing with Deltic (Class 55 diesel-electric) haulage, but the 3,300bhp diesels were unable to operate non-stop over the 393

Taking the place of the Silver Jubilee in the timetable after Nationalisation was the Tees-Tyne Pullman, seen here leaving Darlington behind A4 No 60034 *Lord Faringdon*. This engine carried a double chimney all its life and was still performing well in Scotland in the mid-1960s.
(*RAS Marketing*)

Left: Power for the first down Talisman, the successor to the Coronation's 4.00pm departure time, was provided by A4 No 60025 *Falcon*, which has backed down to King's Cross terminus coupled to an unstreamlined Pacific on 17 September 1956.   (*RAS Marketing*)

A4s were the only locomotives to be entrusted with operating the Elizabethan express non-stop; not even Class 55 Deltic diesel-electrics could power the train without having to make a special stop for crew-changing, in the one year in which they worked the train. Here No 60032 *Gannet* speeds southwards through Croft Spa with the train in 1954.   (*RAS Marketing*)

Sporting BR colours, the A4s carried on their high traditions of operation into post-war days. In this picture, foremost Edinburgh photographer John Robertson has recorded Haymarket stalwart No 60027 *Merlin* leaving Waverley for the Calton North tunnel with the 11.00am Glasgow–King's Cross express.   (*J. Robertson*)

On an overcast morning in the mid-1950s, A4 No 60004 *William Whitelaw* heads the non-stop Elizabethan out of Edinburgh (Waverley) for King's Cross. The 393 mile run posed a considerable operational challenge, particularly in the years 1954–6 as discussed in the accompanying text. (*J. Robertson*)

miles, a service stop being made in Newcastle (Central) in each direction to change crews. The A4s were the only class of locomotives to operate the service non-stop when the time came down to less than seven hours, thanks to their streamlining and their corridor tenders allowing crews to change over in mid-journey. These tenders, which facilitated the service, had been fitted to Gresley's earlier Pacifics, the A1s and A3s, but no representative of either of these classes operated the train in less than 7¼ hours.

In the summers of 1954–56 inclusive, the Elizabethan was run at an average of more than 60mph in 6½ hours. This was 30 minutes faster than the best pre-war (1937–9) timing for a non-stop working, when the load was slightly heavier. Nevertheless this author believes that the operation of the 'non-stop' working – daily and, to a very high degree, punctually – in 1954–56 was the zenith of East Coast working during the age of steam. Although Gresley's earlier Pacifics had operated the service in the summers before 1937 with some distinction, it was the combination of long distance and comparatively heavy load-hauling (frequently around 425 tons gross) at an average of a mile-a-minute over such a distance that made this such an outstanding feat of motive power. Bear in mind that some of the engines involved were in their twentieth year in 1955 – indeed *Silver Link* made forty journeys on this service (at slightly less than 60mph average) in 1961, its 26th year. *Silver Link* was withdrawn the following year, with indecent haste, for no easily discernible reason.

No fewer than nine A4s notched up more than 50

A4 No 60034 *Lord Faringdon* powers the southbound Capitals Limited with nary a wisp of steam or smoke visible in this 1949 shot at Eryholme. At this time the non-stop express between London and Edinburgh was scheduled to take no fewer than eight hours on the journey. (*RAS Marketing*)

Left: In immaculate condition, but lacking any tender markings, A4 No 60031 *Golden Plover* heads an express at an unidentified location (on which the author would welcome advice). (*W. E. Boyd collection*)

Coal is still piled high on the tender of A4 No 60003 *Andrew K. McCosh* as it nears the halfway point of the Capitals Limited run between Edinburgh and London. In this 1950 shot, the locomotive is resplendent in BR blue.   *(RAS Marketing)*

'non-stops' in a season, at least two of them reaching this number on successive days. No 60012 *Commonwealth of Australia*, built for the Coronation service in 1937, is believed to have exceeded 65 such workings, 58 of them consecutively, 20 years after her construction. This roster included weekend balancing workings and were actually non-stop for only five days out of seven, but in its first year *Dominion of New Zealand* operated 62 services, no fewer than 52 of them consecutively, when the train was non-stop six days a week. Obviously, from their earliest years the A4s demonstrated that their streamlining was no gimmick, but an integral part and one reason for their efficient character.

In other words, streamlining had a strong operational *raison d'être*, even when the train services themselves were not streamlined. Without the A4's ability to reduce wind resistance, thus lowering coal consumption, it would surely have been difficult, if not impossible, for the Elizabethan to have operated non-stop on a 6½ hour schedule unless the load had been lightened. Ironically enough, far from working at the limits of their potential on this service in the final period of their careers, the A4s were reckoned by one footplate traveller to have some 20 minutes in hand on the 390 minute schedule between the two capital cities. In the book *Non-Stop!*, this author speculated that there was considerable justification for believing that a six-hour timing would have been perfectly practicable with a lighter load, say no more than nine

Although built for the Coronation service, *Union of South Africa*, seen here in 1950 in its BR guise as No 60009, was a regular post-war performer on the non-stop service between King's Cross and Edinburgh. At that time the service was known as the Capitals Limited, becoming the Elizabethan in 1953. This locomotive headed the last-ever up service to be hauled by steam, in 1961.
(RAS Marketing)

Right: Britain's fastest steam locomotive in post-war times is No 60007 *Sir Nigel Gresley*, whose 112mph in 1959 would have been higher if an inspector had not prevented it. Here this fine Pacific, preserved since 1966 as No 4498, is seen at Cambridge in July 1963 on a tour to commemorate an even faster A4.
(Mike Macdonald collection)

No 60033 *Seagull* was one of the finest A4s, particularly in terms of its performances post-war. The locomotive is seen here at speed at Darlington in 1949, heading south on the non-stop Capitals Limited.   (*RAS Marketing*)

The three-hour Glasgow–Aberdeen services were ideal for A4 operation, with their light loads to be hauled over a well-engineered main line, particularly between Perth and Forfar. No 60024 *Kingfisher* is seen at Stanley junction coming off that section with the 1.30pm Aberdeen–Glasgow in March 1966. The Inverness line curves off to the left.   (*Mitchell Library*)

coaches. And what would that have given? More-or-less a post-war Coronation service, operating in a busy traffic channel with the Flying Scotsman and Junior Scotsman running a few minutes behind it to absorb any excess passengers.

Most admirers of Gresley's A4s, if asked to name an outstanding feat by one of the class in post-war years, would probably nominate the attainment of 112mph down Stoke Bank on 23 May 1959 by No 60007 *Sir Nigel Gresley* on the Stephenson Locomotive Society Golden Jubilee rail tour. This incident could have been all the more momentous but for the fact that an inspector's intervention had prevented Driver Bill Hoole from going for the 1938 record held by *Mallard*. But this was not the only summit of achievement reached by these evergreen engines, whose streamlined casings must have been regarded initially by many traditionally minded railway staff and enthusiasts as a soon-to-be-dismantled aberration. In August 1955, No 60033 *Seagull* made a return journey on the Elizabethan, interspersed with an emergency return trip between King's Cross and Grantham, attaining a revenue-earning mileage of 996 in only 31

After nearly 28 years on Tyneside, No 60016 *Silver King* crossed the Border and performed well on the Scottish Region before withdrawal in March 1965, its 30th year. The locomotive is seen here entering Larbert on a Glasgow (Buchanan Street)–Inverness working not long before withdrawal.   (*Mitchell Library*)

How are the mighty fallen (I). The A4 class had so many suitable candidates for preservation that inevitably many a famous engine went to the scrapheap. No 60014 *Silver Link* was an obvious example, but No 60012 *Commonwealth of Australia* was almost equally illustrious. No 60012 operated 48 out of the first 51 Coronation rosters in 1937, and 19 years later ran more than 65 'non-stop' diagrams between London and Edinburgh in a single summer. The locomotive is seen here in a rather woebegone state at St Margaret's in May 1964.   (*Mitchell Library*)

How are the mighty fallen (II). From the rundown appearance at Polmadie in May 1964, it would be difficult to appreciate that, not long before, No 46228 *Duchess of Rutland* had given O. S. Nock his fastest footplate journey between Crewe and Carlisle on the down Midday Scot. Substituting for a Class 40 diesel-electric at short notice, the Duchess gained nearly ten minutes on schedule, with 455 tons.   (*Mitchell Library*)

hours. Some 80 per cent of this mileage was timed for mile-a-minute running.

The introduction of Class 40 diesel-electrics to the East Coast main line from the 1958/9 winter gave the A4s an unexpected opportunity to shine. With the new machines often failing to maintain rostered diagrams, Gresley's streamlined engines, some of them approaching their quarter-century, were drafted in as substitutes, achieving turnround times that would have amazed pre-war staff. On 18 consecutive working days No 60030 (formerly 4495) completed a return King's Cross–Newcastle journey in only 12 hours, with barely a 2½-hour turnround at Newcastle. Although *Silver Link* accomplished a similar diagram 23 years earlier, providing sole power for the new Silver Jubilee, the A4s might have been expecting to contemplate graceful retirement by this time, instead of averaging 500 miles a day for three weeks.

Not only was the 'non-stop' working trusted exclusively to the A4s, and such new services as the Talisman frequently featured them, as already indicated, but early in the 1960s when a locomotive crisis developed in an area well north of their usual habitat, the East Coast main line, it was the A4s that were sent for.

Class 29 diesels built by the soon to be defunct North British Locomotive Company failed to come up to expectation when used in pairs on the three-hour Glasgow (Buchanan Street)–Aberdeen services. With Class 55 Deltics due to take over an accelerated ECML service in the summer of 1962, it made operational and economic sense for existing express steam power to be given something challenging to carry out. In February 1962, No 60027 *Merlin* hauled a test train on the former Caledonian Glasgow–Aberdeen line within the three hours required. This led to a transfer of A4s now rapidly proving redundant at Haymarket, Nos 60004/9/11/27/31, and they were supplemented the following year by up to nine from south of the border, Nos 60005/6/7/10/16/19/23/26/34. At the height of all this streamlined activity in the unlikely setting of Strathmore and over the hills of Kinbuck and Gleneagles, the following A4s were allocated to these workings by 1 July 1964:

At Aberdeen (Ferryhill); Nos 60004/6/7/9/10/12/16/19/23/26/34.

At Glasgow (St Rollox); Nos 60027/31.

Nos 60005/11 had also operated from Ferryhill but were already withdrawn by 1964, while the allocation of No 60016 to this former Caledonian depot is of some interest. This was *Silver King*, built in the autumn of 1935 as the third of the original four intended to power the Silver Jubilee. No 60016 spent the first 28 years of its life on Tyneside before moving north and operating for a further 18 months from Aberdeen (after a brief sojourn in Edinburgh). In view of its origin, *Silver King* might well have made a more suitable preservation candidate than at least one of the other A4s which was saved from the scrapheap.

The record of performance of the streamlined A4s on the Glasgow–Aberdeen trains is unfortunately somewhat nebulous. A 75mph speed ceiling existed on the line at the time, and no sooner had Cecil J. Allen published, in May 1965, an account of a southbound run by No 60034 *Lord Faringdon*, including a 21.7 mile dash reeled off at an average of 82.6mph, than he was advised by a Scottish Region official that his published log could land the crew in trouble, containing as it did fourteen speed 'infringements'. Allen later admitted in an article in *Modern Railways* (January 1966) that he had quite deliberately suppressed later logs of interest for this very reason. How ironic that a class of locomotives which was introduced in such secrecy in 1935 should exit from the railway scene 30 years later in similar circumstances! But what a pity that more is not known of the work of these veteran engines, working trains of very similar weight to those they were first introduced to haul.

All this was a magnificent testimony to the high reputation enjoyed by these locomotives, particularly since their LMS rivals, the Duchess Class 8P Pacifics, were to be denied any such late flowering. The 24 streamlined members of that class had their streamlining removed by 1949 thus making them, in theory at least, easier to maintain, while a number of the class were constructed up to nine years after the last A4.

The former LNER streamlined Pacifics achieved an average lifespan of 27 years, almost exactly three years longer than their LMS rivals, and that despite the fact that a number of the King's Cross engines – including *Silver Link* and *Seagull* – were withdrawn at the end of 1962, when they surely had a few years left in them. Two of the class, *Silver King* and *Kingfisher*, came within a couple of months of celebrating their 30th anniversaries, while the shortest-lived A4 (all this excludes No 4469 destroyed by the Luftwaffe) was No 4902, withdrawn as No 60033. Incredibly, the 'youngest' to be withdrawn was arguably the best of the whole class. In other words, even though the A4s did not enjoy particularly preferential treatment south of the Scottish border in the 1960s, they still achieved greater average longevity than the Duchesses. As already suggested in the chapter on the Coronation Scot – and this is purely author's speculation – the inferior water capacity of the latters' tenders surely reduced their effectiveness on lines away from the West Coast main line.

The last of these comparatively high-speed Scottish trains were entrusted to the A4s in 1966, after which the last two operational examples, Nos 60019 and 60024 were withdrawn. The former became one of the six of the class to be preserved, being somewhat incongruously disguised in 1988 as the non-surviving *Silver Link*.

Admirers of Bulleid's Southern Pacifics will no doubt be quick to point out that those machines continued to run on the Waterloo–Bournemouth line until even later than this, but the point about the A4s' Scottish running was that they were specially allocated to the traffic, on a line over which they would not normally work, and were preferred to diesel motive power more than 20 years their junior.

Two A4s were left in normal revenue-earning service in 1966, one being No 60024, the other No 60019 *Bittern*. The latter is seen here at Aberdeen in April 1966, still capable of fascinating a younger generation. Unlike No 60024, *Bittern* was purchased by admirers from North East England, where the locomotive had spent most of its working life, but is now preserved somewhat fictionally as No 2509 *Silver Link*. (*Mitchell Library*)

POSTSCRIPT

A CRITICAL LOOK AT BRITAIN'S STREAMLINED TRAINS

LNER

To the rail enthusiast, any train which is designed to capture the public's imagination by travelling faster than anything before – and does so – must be a success. To the historian, a more circumspect approach is required. By the end of the 1930s Britain's railways had four streamlined services operating, with six train sets. Both the LNER Coronation and LMS Coronation Scot were operated by two sets simultaneously; the Silver Jubilee and West Riding Limited consisted of one set undertaking journeys each way. There was also a spare set on standby on both East and West main lines. It is arguable that the East Anglian was not a streamlined service (certainly its stock was not) but if it is included, then the LNER had accumulated a total of four streamlined passenger services daily achieving 1,952 miles. This was not far short of 10,000 miles of high-speed travel weekly.

Michael Bonavia believes (see the Bibliography) that the LNER's introduction of steam-powered streamlined services into Britain, in preference to diesel power, postponed the inevitable re-equipment of Britain's railways with more modern means of motive power. But it could be argued that the really appropriate opportunity for such a re-utilisation came not before World War II but after it. In the 1930s the adaptation of a steam engine to haul streamlined services was an easy one, and remarkably successful. Gresley's A4s were good at their job, involved no basic crew re-training or the use of imported

The 'drawing power' of steam is not just expressed in horsepower, as is evident from the admiring group round No 60022 *Mallard*, when on ordinary passenger duties at Doncaster in 1959. (*Mitchell Library*)

fuels, and could be rostered to handle other traffic down to and including goods trains if required. To introduce diesels at that time would probably have involved dislocation in motive power departments throughout the country, while (assuming the purchase of German equipment) placing some degree of dependence on a nation soon to become an enemy.

The streamlined train broke away from, indeed, totally inverted, the LNER's existing policy of providing over-capacity for its potential passengers in the shape of 14 or 15 coaches on its express trains when ten might suffice. At the beginning of the 1930s there had been comment both inside and outside the company on this over-provision of vehicles, which was operational policy. In 1933, in a report made directly to Wedgwood, the chief general manager, a traffic apprentice named L. W. Ibbotson commented specifically on this over-capacity. He personally sampled a number of trains to assess the quality of the LNER's service and found it necessary to point out the number of trains conveying more Third class vehicles than the traffic could possibly warrant. Had his comments been acted upon this would have undermined one of the cornerstones of LNER passenger train policy and its ensuing motive power requirements before World War II. After all, the *raison d'être* of the Gresley and Raven Pacifics had been to answer the need for a locomotive to haul 500 ton trains at 60mph. To point out that few expresses needed to load regularly to much more than 350 tons was probably sacrilege!

A typical northbound express out of King's Cross in 1928, for example, would consist of 15 coaches bound for no fewer than six destinations. The 4.00pm departure in pre-Coronation days conveyed four vehicles for Leeds and one for Bradford, detached from the five-coach York and Scarborough section (including the two restaurant cars) at Doncaster. Four vehicles for Cleethorpes, and one for Horncastle, were also detached en route. Geoff

Goslin, writing in the *Gresley Observer*, has pointed out that, complicated though all this was, the corresponding up journey, involving coupling-up and regaining brake vacuum, was likely to be even more time-consuming. All this so the LNER could advertise through connections to the destinations concerned, when faster and lighter direct services, with passengers changing where necessary, would probably have served the public better.

Ibbotson's comments were vociferously opposed by the passenger superintendents' committee, arguing that an under-used coaching rake running in one direction might well be full to capacity on the return journey. What this entailed in unnecessary fuel consumption and lubrication, not to mention human toil, was not quantified. The only occasion when criticism of this policy surfaced in the technical press was when a company fireman wrote to one of the magazines deploring the extra muscle-power necessary to hand-fuel express steam locomotives:

> 'For a fireman to have to heave coal into these monsters when trailing enormous trains of 30-ton to 34-ton bogies about, with a few passengers in each, is a heart-breaking job.'

As indicated earlier, the streamlined services represented an inversion of this over-capacity policy by *limiting* the number of passengers allowed in the train. In theory, the Pullman services had also done this, but obviously were not catering for the average traveller. Michael Bonavia, while harbouring strong reservations about the powering of the streamlined trains by steam, does concede that

> 'there was much to be said for exploiting human technology to the full and gaining immense prestige and publicity value from steam trains

which were an advance on anything previously available and whose romantic appeal can still affect us today'.

This author is inclined to question just how much of an advance the British streamlined trains actually were; their conservatism in design and use of materials was disappointing and less innovative than it might have been, but the reader will no doubt wish to make up his or her own mind on this point.

Nevertheless, there seems no doubt that the LNER's streamlined expresses were a commercial success, particularly the Silver Jubilee. In his informal history of the LNER, Dr Bonavia quotes revenue from all four of the company's streamlined services, for a four-week period ending 9 July 1938, as follows:

Train	Gross £	Net £	Costs %	Mileage	Profit/train mile £ (net)
Silver Jubilee	8,261	6,977	15	10,720	£0.65
Coronation	12,748	10,730	15	15,720	£0.68
West Riding	4,875	3,936	19	7,400	£0.53
East Anglian	1,840	1,399	23	4,600	£0.30

Calculations of profit over costs, and revenue per train mile are made by this author, and any error contained therein is his responsibility entirely.

From the above figures it can be seen that the Coronation earned the most while incurring the highest costs. The first three trains were new services, presumably generating new traffic, while the fourth was a conventional train and might conceivably have earned much the same revenue total had it not been streamlined (or semi-streamlined, to be more accurate). Its costs deductions were the lowest, and, as Dr Bonavia's figures do not appear to include 'first cost', was by far the cheapest to implement. The Coronation must have been something of a disappointment, comprising as it did two train sets and the novelty of observation cars.

Certainly there are grounds for wondering if the LNER had properly thought through its Coronation express concept with due care, or had perhaps become overconfident in the commercial prospects of streamlining. A letter-writer (R. A. H. Weight) to a rail magazine during the December previous to the train's introduction had sagely pointed out that Edinburgh was an entirely different kind of destination from Newcastle. The Scottish capital did not have the same size of business community as Newcastle – and the latter conurbation had twice the population – while businessmen and professional people in Edinburgh were simply not accustomed to contemplating regular trips to and from London without making at least one or both journeys overnight.

Not the least reason for this was the 1896 agreement between East and West Coast rail companies to keep speeds down on Anglo-Scottish services, in case of a recurrence of racing. The fact that this quite informal arrangement, effectively a cartel against the public interest, remained in force until 1932 was a black mark against both LNER and LMS; the former company paid dearly for it when it introduced its Coronation express. With the 1896 agreement only laid to rest five years earlier, at least ten years later than it should have been, there had been insufficient time for the company to build up a *regular* travelling clientele between the capitals.

Not only that, but Edinburgh's position as a route centre (Waverley is a through station as well as a terminal) complicated the traffic equation to be considered. There should ideally have been as early an arrival in Edinburgh and as late a departure as possible for daytime trains, to facilitate connections to and from Glasgow, Dundee, Aberdeen, Perth and perhaps even Inverness. In fact the train's own souvenir booklet specified only two services connecting with the 10.00pm arrival – the 10.15pm to Kirkcaldy and 10.30pm to Glasgow (Queen Street). Thus the timing of the down Coronation reduced the number of destinations north of Edinburgh that could easily be reached before midnight – Dundee and Aberdeen for example, could not, nor the university town and tourist centre of St Andrews – while the light loadings on the northern section of the northbound run showed that there was little or no business traffic to cater for at that time in the late evening. A morning departure in the down direction and return from Scotland in the late afternoon would have been worth trying. This would have required only one coaching set, had roller bearings been fitted. Equally, a 1.30pm departure from King's Cross would have made possible an arrival at Aberdeen before 11.00pm; ironically, this was the departure time of the rival Coronation Scot which ran into its northern terminus with no long-distance connections available to mesh with its 8.00pm arrival time.

Alternatively, the existing Coronation trains should simply have been extended to Glasgow in order to give an earlier arrival time there than the existing one of 11.39pm, including a 30-minute wait at Waverley. Arrival at Queen Street station could easily have been accomplished at 11.00pm, assuming seven minutes to change engines in the down direction at Edinburgh, and 53 minutes allowed for the 47 miles on to Glasgow. A 4.00pm departure from London for Glasgow might well have been very attractive to business passengers – 2½ hours extra in the capital would have been quite a bonus for a Glaswegian businessman, bought at the expense of only an extra 30 minutes in a train. Fifty-five minutes would have been allowed for the up train between Glasgow and Edinburgh, including the climb of Cowlairs Bank, but there would have been time to take water or change engines at Waverley, or at Newcastle – the up train was, as we know, an easier proposition for the engine.

Even without a double return trip, the Coronation's mileage was nearly double that of the East Anglian which, as already observed, spent barely four hours in revenue-earning service in every 24, totalling 20 hours per week. It is difficult to understand why a double return London–Norwich trip could not have been rostered, up from Norwich at about 8.00am, back down as a noon departure from Liverpool Street, up again at about 3.30pm, returning not much more than half an hour later in the evening than the actual 6.40pm departure.

* * *

With the 20-20 vision granted by hindsight, it is interesting to look critically in retrospect at the physical design of the LNER's three streamlined expresses. The locomotives are not included in this appraisal – the A4s built new for the three train services outlasted them in everyday traffic, in the case of some individual locomotives, by more than a quarter of a century, while the B17s came from a class that had already several years' traffic experience under its belt by the time the first streamliner ran.

The first critical point to be made about the LNER streamlined trains was their apparent waste of space. The Silver Jubilee carried two restaurant cars, the Coronation two kitchen cars, while each conveyed two guard's vans. Yet these were intended to be exclusive, short, fast, expresses, supposedly Britain's answer to the original German *Fliegende Hamburger* which packed half as many passengers into a quarter of the number of coaches!

Norman Bel Geddes, in designing his 1931 concept of his Streamlined (Railway) Car No 4, commented 'First consideration has been given to comfort and convenience of passengers rather than maximum capacity.'

Gresley might have written these words himself; his first two streamlined trains were certainly not designed intensively. The Silver Jubilee perpetuated the idea of keeping First and Third class diners well apart, separated by the kitchen car, while it seems absurd for a comparatively short lightweight super-express such as the Coronation to carry two kitchen cars and two guard's vans. Even worse in this respect was the six-coach East Anglian, which also had two brake vans, as well as preserving the social apartheid of feeding First and Third class passengers separately. Indeed, here were only two coaches, one for each class, exclusively devoted to the basic purpose of providing passenger accommodation!

The Coronation incorporated the Pullman-type concept of meals 'at seat', at least eliminating the double restaurant cars, but not the second guard's van. In view of the concept of exclusivity epitomised by these trains, surely it would have been logical to make the formation of the Jubilee one class – perhaps Third with a supplementary fare, the whole package wrapped up as 'Business' or 'Executive' class, with 'at seat' catering. This would have released valuable space for increased seating by elimination of both restaurant cars. As for the supernumerary seats in the Coronation's observation cars – these faintly mirrored Bel Geddes' idea of a lounge scarcely practical within the British loading gauge – but consideration could have been given to seating passengers there throughout the journey, paying an extra supplement to First-class fare.

With their short, steel-panelled, bodies built on teak, Gresley's streamlined coaches were hardly revolutionary in design. They were some 3½ft shorter than many standard British vehicles of the period; surely the use of aluminium (first employed on British railway coaching stock 25 years previously) and lightweight steel would have allowed a longer body without loss of strength or any great increase in tare weight. Some six or eight extra passengers could have been accommodated in each coach without compromising on comfort.

Bel Geddes anticipated Gresley in predicting elasticated sheeting between coaches, and an observation car with sloping windows. But there was no turning by the LNER to lightweight metals such as aluminium for coach bodies, no special bogies, no roller bearings. In one sense, the LNER's streamlined expresses were superficial in the concept and character of their streamlining, embodying, in the coaching stock at least, fairly conservative values. This superficiality was particularly paper-thin in the case

of the East Anglian, with its token streamline casing for its B17 locomotive, and externally conventional stock. (The LMS's Coronation Scot, with its almost conventional stock and comparatively slow schedule, is deserving of separate consideration and criticism later in this chapter.)

As to the interior decor of Gresley's coaching stock, its appeal is subject to the vagaries of personal taste. One point that seems indisputable is that the Silver Jubilee interiors were traditional in appearance, in total contrast to the trend on the other side of the Atlantic for streamlined services to have furnishing and tables with clean unfussy lines. The LNER's streamlined stock was offering virtual Pullman comfort (particularly in the Coronation with its meals served at the passengers' seats), but 'streamlined' internally? Hardly.

Gresley must have been aware that the London–Newcastle services were well-patronised anyway, and that 'streamlined' decor would appear gimmicky to an established clientele. The Jubilee's patrons were being tempted away from existing LNER services, rather than from any aircraft or road competitors, so traditional decor and seating was only appropriate. It should also be remembered that by 1935 Gresley had been responsible for all rolling stock – from a coal wagon to an express passenger locomotive – on two of Britain's most important railways for a quarter of a century (GNR 1911–23, LNER 1923–41). Such an established member of the British engineering fraternity would be unlikely to slavishly copy an American style of interior coach decor.

Any disappointment felt about the coaching stock is in contrast to Gresley's express locomotives, whose designs had shown a progressive innovatory process since the production of the 'Hush-Hush' 4–6–4 in 1929. His caution in coach design could be defended in 1935 in that he was answering an operational challenge to build at fairly short notice a revenue-earning train, without the benefit of a research and development department to provide intensive technical studies, and without being able to entertain the flights of fancy which a freelance designer could.

* * *

World War II prevented a second generation of streamliners from being built, and one is tempted to let the imagination loose speculating on what might have been. Lightweight coaching-stock with aluminium 68ft long bodies on steel frames and roller bearings would

surely have given the A4s an even lighter load to haul, probably not more than 155 tons gross. Articulated stock need not have been necessary if greater body length had been likely to cause problems on the curves north of Newcastle. Five such lightweight coaches, with the middle coach accommodating guard, kitchen, staff resting quarters (two locomotive crews and two guards would be carried, probably along with four waiters and three kitchen staff) and cocktail bar, would seat up to 192 passengers (four coaches seating 48 passengers each). Meals would be served 'at seat', and one of the coaches could be an observation car for which passengers paid a special extra supplement, or were allocated seats there on request on a 'first come, first served' basis for the entire journey.

Fitted with roller bearings, this train could have offered a Glasgow–London service in little more than 6½ hours – by LNER. A stop would be made at Edinburgh only, leaving Glasgow (Queen Street) at 7.15am, Waverley at 8.05am, then running into King's Cross at 1.50pm. Return would be at 4.45pm, arriving Glasgow at 11.20pm. Footplate crews would change through the corridor tender approximately 50 miles south of Newcastle. Admittedly this timetabling reflected post-war traffic patterns, with an evening departure from London proving more popular for Scottish travellers than before 1939. But, in view of figures quoted earlier in this chapter, perhaps it was the West Riding that was the potential growth market – Bradford and Wakefield could have been given their own streamliner, quite independent of Harrogate and Leeds.

LMS

If criticism of the LNER's streamlined trains is valid – and none of it is based on information not known to the railway administrators at the time – then such criticism is redoubled when the LMS Coronation Scot is considered.

The stock is open to the same criticism as that of the rival LNER – there was an enormous waste of space. Again, there were two kitchen cars and two brakes, while the average length of each coach was around 57ft. The kitchen cars were no more than 50ft in length, although the First class diner was 65ft. Coaches 70ft long had already been introduced on the GWR, so criticism of their stock for the Coronation Scot is surely justified. Not only was new stock not constructed for a long-awaited service, but the existing rake was not even the most modern stock in design terms.

The point has already been made that this was a company riven by conflict between its constituent companies, so a new glamour service could have had almost as beneficial an effect on staff morale as on customer relations, justifying greater investment. If Messrs Essery and Jenkinson are correct in suggesting that the LMS coaching stock was more modern in outline than the LNER's, then the Coronation Scot's rake was even more regrettable, since in a sense the LMS had less far to go to achieve a truly impressive production. Nine coaches to transport only 233 passengers was hardly cost-effective, yet the LMS made it obvious by its refusal to construct new stock that economy was an important factor. From a distance the lack of streamlined fairing on the underframes was a disappointment, and this despite the fact that the company had possessed data on the resistance of under-carriage fittings for some years.

The average speed of the Coronation Scot was, as already observed, a let-down at the time. Even if the operating authorities were being cautious in allowing 390 minutes for the 401 miles, when an unstreamlined Pacific had already hauled eight coaches over the distance in 345 minutes, there would surely have been potential for tightening the time when running experience had been gained, as one official hinted to a journalist in June 1937. After all, the LNER's test run for the Silver Jubilee in March 1935 had shown that a 233 minute timing was possible over 268 miles; the schedule subsequently introduced was only seven minutes slower. The difference of some 45 minutes between the LMS test run by No 6201 *Princess Elizabeth* in November 1936 and the schedule subsequently put into effect was surely unnecessary if operating alternatives had been examined.

Since an LMS corridor-tender was constructed at this time, it certainly appears that the company was aware of the possibilities opened-up by running the 401 miles non-stop. This would have saved at least eight minutes on the schedule, and would have created a long-distance non-stopping record on a regular service – records are the oxygen of publicity, something a streamlined train needed

if it was to thrive. Equally, a corridor tender would have allowed a stop for the down service on the outskirts of Glasgow to allow a connection with the Perth portion of the Midday Scot, thus giving convenient access to Gleneagles, the location of one of the LMS's best hotels, and a destination specially illustrated in the train's introductory brochure distributed to the American public.

But this raises a point about where the Coronation Scot's clientele was expected to come from. This author has already suggested that the LNER's Coronation should have been extended to and from Glasgow because of unsatisfactory patronage of the down service. Effectively, the LNER was offering a businessman's service to and from Edinburgh, which was a tourist, not a commercial, centre. The LMS was squaring the equation by offering a service timed for the casual traveller to and from a northern destination which was simply not an attraction for tourists. Glasgow was not then the cultural centre it is now; indeed, the LMS did not even illustrate it in the train's introductory brochure for the US tourist market.

On the other hand, such an industrial city would probably be prepared to patronise a train offering, say, a 4.00pm or 4.15pm departure from Euston, particularly if there were ticketing incentives for an overnight journey up from Glasgow the previous evening. Operationally too, there would have been scope for a morning up service from Glasgow, arriving at Euston at about 2.30pm, although roller bearings would have had to be fitted. Obviously a Coronation Scot set making two daily journeys between the cities would probably have earned enough to justify the construction of new stock – and specially-*designed* stock at that – in the first place. Bear in mind that, if any of this critical appraisal seems captious, the LMS itself had more than 18 months to observe streamlined workings on another British line before taking the plunge.

While there is no evidence that the Coronation Scot's loading figures were disappointing, the fact remained that the company was offering a fast service, likely to appeal to the business market, at a departure time long associated with a heavy omnibus express which was not particularly fast but offered a reasonable service to the

holidaymaker or casual traveller. The Midday Scot offered connections to and from Aberdeen, Perth, Edinburgh, the Lancashire cities of Liverpool and Manchester, and even attached a Penzance coach at Crewe to and from northern destinations. The introduction of the Coronation Scot did not change any of this, merely creaming off the Euston–Glasgow through passengers, but the LMS was still obliged to offer a Glasgow section on the following train for passengers joining at intermediate stations.

The established pattern of midday departures would not have been disturbed if the Coronation Scot had been introduced as it should have been, as a late afternoon departure from both cities. This would have served the business traveller and would hopefully have *created* a new market, as a streamlined service was supposed to do. It would have pre-empted any Glasgow-ward extension of the LNER's Coronation which could not have competed with even the 6½ hour schedule, while there would still have been scope for northbound passengers to catch up with the Aberdeen portion of the Midday Scot at around Law Junction, if desired. As it was, the 1.35pm ex-Euston following the new Coronation Scot was into Glasgow at 9.55pm; with an accelerated schedule a retimed streamliner could have left Euston at 4.15pm, 165 minutes later than its existing departure time and only have been 35 minutes later into Glasgow than the existing alternative. There would have been no need for a Glasgow section on the Midday Scot as the Aberdeen section of the train, if retimed out of Euston at (say) 2.15pm, and overtaken by the streamliner at or near Carstairs, could have picked up Coronation Scot travellers for Gleneagles at Law Junction, while the following express would exchange its Glasgow-bound passengers, collected at intermediate stops, to a specially-timed local from Law to Glasgow. All this is assuming that the new streamliner made a non-stop, or at least a fast, run from London to Law.

All this speculation may be the product of imagination, but it was imagination that started and sustained the public appetite for things streamlined, from domestic irons to railway trains.

BIBLIOGRAPHY

BOOKS

Allen, Cecil J. *British Pacific Locomotives*. Ian Allan, 2nd edn, 1971.

Bannister, Eric *Trained by Sir Nigel Gresley*. Dalesman, 1984.

Bennet, A. R. *The First Railway in London*. 1912.

Bonavia, M. R. *A History of the LNER*. Vol. II. *The Age of the Streamliners, 1934–39*. Allen & Unwin, 1982.

Brown, F. A. S. *Nigel Gresley*. Ian Allan, 1961.

Clay, J. F. & Cliffe, J. *The West Coast Pacifics*. Ian Allan, 1976.

Collier, Robert (3rd Baron Monkswell). *Railways of Great Britain*. Smith Elder, 1913.

— *Railways*. Benn, 1928.

Conway, Hugh. *Bugatti*. Octopus Books, 1984.

Day-Lewis, Sean. *Bulleid: Last Giant of Steam*. Allen & Unwin, 1964.

Essery, R. J. & Jenkinson, D. *The LMS Coach*. Ian Allan, 1969.

Geddes, Norman Bel. *Horizons*. 1934.

Gourvish, T. R. *British Railways 1948–1973: A Business History*. CUP, 1987.

Haresnape, B. *Design for Steam 1830–1960*. 2nd edn. Ian Allan, 1981.

— *Gresley Locomotives: A Pictorial History*. Ian Allan, 1981.

— *Railway Design Since 1830*. Ian Allan, 1968.

Harris, M. *Gresley's Coaches*. David & Charles, 1973.

Hillier, Bevis. *The Style of the Century, 1900–1980*. Herbert Press, 1983.

Jenkinson, D. *British Railway Carriages of the Twentieth Century*, II. Patrick Stephens, 1990.

Jenkinson, D. & Essery, R. J. *Locomotive Liveries of the LMS*. Ian Allan, 1967.

Loewy, Raymond. *Industrial Design*. 1980.

— *The Locomotive: its Aesthetics*. 1937.

London Midland & Scottish Railway. *'Coronation Scot' Touring the USA*. 1937.

— *LMS Research Laboratory, Derby*. (Souvenir Brochure, 1935)

— *The Track of the 'Coronation Scot'*. 1937.

London & North Eastern Railway. *The 'Coronation'*. 1937.

Marshall, C. F. Dendy. *The Resistance of Express Trains*. Railway Engineer (monograph), 1925.

Mullay, A. J. *Non-Stop!: London to Scotland Steam*. Sutton, 1989.

Nock, O. S. *Speed Records on British Railways*. David & Charles, 1971.

— *The Locomotives of Sir Nigel Gresley*. Longmans, 1945.

— *Sir William Stanier: An Engineering Biography*. Ian Allan, 1964.

Railway Correspondence & Travel Society. *Locomotives of the LNER*. Parts 2A, 2B.

— *Locomotives of the GWR*. Part 8, 2nd edn, 1960.

Rankine, William M. *A Manual of the Steam Engine and Other Prime Movers*. Griffin, 1859.

Reed, Robert C. *The Streamline Era*. Golden West Books, 1975.

Rogers, H. C. B. *Chapelon: Genius of French Steam*. Ian Allan, 1972.

Rowledge, J. W. P. *The LMS Pacifics*. David & Charles, 1987.

Self, Alan. 'Streamlined Expresses of the LNER'. In *Design History; Fad or Function*. Design Council, 1978.

Stroud, John. *Railway Air Services*. Ian Allan, 1987.

Townend, P. N. *East Coast Pacifics at Work*. Ian Allan, 1982.

Vuillet, G. *Railway Reminiscences of Three Continents*. Nelson, 1968.

Webster, H. C. *2750, Legend of a Locomotive*. Nelson, 1953.

Yeadon, H. B. *Yeadon's Register of LNER Locomotives*, II. Irwell, 1990.

ARCHIVES

SRO Files   BR/LNE/8/340. (1935 High Speed Trials)

      BR/LNE/8/359. (Daily reports on the running of The Coronation and patronage afforded)

      BR/LNE/8/387. (1946 Trials)

      LNER Staff Circular 298.

      LNER Circular AD40/1946.

      LNER report on Express Trains by L. W. Ibbotson, 1933.

PERIODICAL ARTICLES

Aspinall, John A. F. 'Train Resistance'. In *Proceedings of the Institution of Civil Engineers*, Vol. 147, 1901, pp. 155–277.

Butterfield, M. 'Grouping, Practice and Competition: the Passenger Policy of the LNER, 1923–39'. In *Journal of Transport History*, 3rd series, Vol. 7, 1986, pp. 21–47.

Gresley, H. N. 'Address by the President'. In *Proceedings of the Institution of Mechanical Engineers*, Vol. 133, 1936, pp. 251–65.

Gresley Observer. Various articles – 'Papyrus: Account [of run on March 5th 1935] and Comments' by John Aylard (issue 76, 1985). Reminiscences of Drivers Haygreen (86, 1988), Maguire (81, 1986), Peachey (76, 1985), and Taylor (77, 1985). 'Silver Jubilee Trip in 1936' by Michael Joyce (81, 1986). 'A Train Fire at Huntingdon' [July 14th 1951] by Geoff Goslin (97, 1992).

Johansen, F. C. 'The Air Resistance of Passenger Trains'. In *Proceedings of the Institution of Mechanical Engineers*, Vol. 134, 1936, pp. 91–208.

Lardner, Dionysius. 'First report on the determination of the mean numerical values of railway constraints.' In *Report of the British Association for the Advancement of Science*, 1838, pp. 197–252.

— 'Second and concluding report on the determination of the mean value of railway constraints'. In *Report of the British Association for the Advancement of Science*, 1841, pp. 205–47.

Neve, E. 'The Last LNER Luxury Expresses'. In *Railway World*, October 1987, pp. 614–7.

Newsome, N. 'The Development of LNER Carriage and Wagon Design, 1923–41'. In *Proceedings of the Institution of Locomotive Engineers*, Vol. 38, 1948, pp. 420–83.

Spencer, B. 'Development of LNER Locomotives'. In *Proceedings of the Institution of Locomotive Engineers*, Vol. 37, 1947.

Stanier, W. A. 'Recent Developments in Locomotive Design'. *Proceedings of the Institution of Mechanical Engineers*. Vol. 133, 1936, pp. 553–94.

Wagner, R. P. 'High Speed and the Steam Locomotive'. In *Proceedings of the Institution of Mechanical Engineers*, Vol. 124, 1935.

Also various articles in: *Annual Reports of the National Physical Laboratory, Backtrack, Glasgow Herald, LNER Magazine, Modern Railways, Newcastle Journal, Railway Gazette, Railway Magazine, Railway Observer, Scotsman, The Times*.

TABLE E
At-a-glance Table of British Streamlined Trains, 1935–9
(With outstanding contemporary trains listed below for comparison)

Name of train	Company	Introduced	Between	No of stops	Average speed (mph)
Silver Jubilee	LNER	9/35	King's Cross–Newcastle	1	66.9
Coronation	LNER	7/37	King's Cross–Edinburgh	1 up / 2 down	65.4
Coronation Scot	LMS	7/37	Euston–Glasgow (Central)	1	61.6
West Riding Ltd	LNER	9/37	King's Cross–Leeds/Bradford	0	63.3
Bristolian	GWR	9/35	Paddington–Bristol	0	67.6
Fliegende Hamburger (Germany)		1933	Berlin–Hamburg	1	76.9
Fliegende Kölner (Germany)		1935	Berlin–Cologne	2	70.5
Hiawatha (US)		1935	Chicago–St Paul	6	63.2

TABLE F
Chronology of Streamlined Steam Services, 1923–39

GREAT BRITAIN		ABROAD	GREAT BRITAIN		ABROAD
	1923		LNER Silver Jubilee trial	27 September	
Formation of LMS & LNER	1 January		LNER Silver Jubilee service	30 September	
	1931			**1936**	
		Brill cars on Philadelphia & Western (USA)		15 July	Mercury, NYC
			LNER 113mph on Silver Jubilee	27 August	
	1933			**1937**	
	15 May	Fliegende Hamburger (Germany)	LMS attains 114mph	29 June	
	1934		LMS Coronation Scot	5 July	
	1 November	Asia Express (Manchuria)	LNER Coronation	5 July	
LNER London–Leeds speed trial	30 November		LNER West Riding	27 September	
			LNER East Anglian	27 September	
	1935			**1938**	
	January	Commodore Vanderbilt, NYC (USA)	LNER attains 126mph	3 July	
LNER London–Newcastle trial	5 March				
	29 May	Hiawatha, Milwaukee RR (USA)		**1939**	
	1 July	Fliegende Kölner (Germany)	LNER streamline services cease	31 August	
	Summer	PLM Streamliner (France)	Outbreak of World War II	3 September	
GWR Bristolian	9 September				

TABLE G
British Steam Locomotives built/rebuilt for Streamlined Services 1935–1943

GENERAL NOTES

1 Name changes are omitted, unless they took place before 1939, and after the locomotive left Works.
2 The LNER streamlined W1 4–6–4 (from 1937) and the P2 2–8–2s are excluded from these tables as they were not designed to work specific named passenger services.
3 'P' after withdrawal dates indicates preserved locomotives.

LONDON & NORTH EASTERN RAILWAY (LNER) CLASS A4 4–6–2

All were built streamlined, and apart from valancing removed, retained streamlining when withdrawn from service.

Date	No	Name	Service for which built	Withdrawn
9/35	2509	Silver Link	Silver Jubilee	12/62
9/35	2510	Quicksilver	,,	4/63
11/35	2511	Silver King	,,	3/65
12/35	2512	Silver Fox	,,	10/63
12/36	4482	Golden Eagle	(General)	10/64
12/36	4483	Kingfisher	,,	9/66
2/37	4484	Falcon	,,	10/63
2/37	4485	Kestrel	,,	12/65
3/37	4486	Merlin	,,	9/65
4/37	4487	Sea Eagle	,,	12/62
6/37	4488	Union of South Africa	Coronation	6/66P
5/37	4489	Woodcock/ Dominion of Canada	,,	5/65P
6/37	4490	Empire of India	,,	5/64
6/37	4491	Commonwealth of Australia	,,	8/64
6/37	4492	Dominion of New Zealand	,,	4/63
7/37	4493	Woodcock	(General)	10/63
8/37	4494	Osprey	,,	12/62
8/37	4495	Great Snipe/ Golden Fleece	West Riding Ltd	12/62
9/37	4496	Golden Shuttle	,,	7/63P
10/37	4497	Golden Plover	(General)	10/65
11/37	4498	Sir Nigel Gresley	,,	2/66P
11/37	4462	Great Snipe	,,	7/66
12/37	4463	Sparrow Hawk	,,	6/63
12/37	4464	Bittern	,,	9/66P
12/37	4465	Guillemot	,,	3/64
1/38	4466	Herring Gull	,,	9/65
2/38	4467	Wild Swan	,,	10/63
3/38	4468	Mallard	,,	4/63P
3/38	4469	Gadwall/Sir Ralph Wedgwood	,,	6/42
4/38	4499	Pochard/Sir Murrough Wilson	,,	5/64
4/38	4500	Garganey/Sir Ronald Matthews	,,	10/64
5/38	4900	Gannet	,,	10/63
6/38	4901	Capercaillie	,,	3/64
6/38	4902	Seagull	,,	12/62
7/38	4903	Peregrine	,,	8/66

LONDON & NORTH EASTERN RAILWAY (LNER) CLASS B17/5 4–6–0

Date	No	Name	Service for which rebuilt	Date stream-lined	Stream-lining removed	With-drawn
6/36	2859	East Anglian	East Anglian	9/37	4/51	3/60
5/37	2870	City of London	East Anglian	9/37	4/51	4/60

No 2859 originally Norwich City
No 2870 originally Manchester City, then Tottenham Hotspur

LONDON MIDLAND & SCOTTISH RAILWAY (LMS) CLASS 7P (later 8P) PRINCESS CORONATION 4–6–2 (ALTERNATIVELY "DUCHESS" CLASS)

All were built streamlined – this feature was removed as shown below. Nos 6220–6229 were built for the Coronation Scot service; Nos 6235–6248 were built for general service.

Date	No	Name	Streamlining removed	Withdrawn
5/37	6220	Coronation	3/47	4/63
6/37	6221	Queen Elizabeth	5/46	5/63
6/37	6222	Queen Mary	5/46	10/63
7/37	6223	Princess Alice	8/46	10/63
7/37	6224	Princess Alexandra	5/46	10/63
5/38	6225	Duchess of Gloucester	3/47	9/64
5/38	6226	Duchess of Norfolk	10/48	9/64
6/38	6227	Duchess of Devonshire	8/46	12/62
6/38	6228	Duchess of Rutland	11/47	9/64
9/38	6229	Duchess of Hamilton	1/48	2/64P
7/39	6235	City of Birmingham	4/46	9/64P
7/39	6236	City of Bradford	12/47	3/64
8/39	6237	City of Bristol	1/47	9/64
9/39	6238	City of Carlisle	8/46	9/64
9/39	6239	City of Chester	9/47	9/64
3/40	6240	City of Coventry	7/47	9/64
4/40	6241	City of Edinburgh	1/47	9/64
5/40	6242	City of Glasgow	4/47	10/63
6/40	6243	City of Lancaster	5/49	9/64
7/40	6244	King George VI*	8/47	9/64
6/43	6245	City of London	10/47	9/64
8/43	6246	City of Manchester	10/46	1/63
9/43	6247	City of Liverpool	1/47	5/63
10/43	6248	City of Leeds	12/46	9/64

* City of Leeds until April 1941

TABLE H
BR/LNER and LNER/BR Cross Indices – Numbers of Streamlined Locomotives

BR	LNER	LNER	BR
60001	4500	2509	60014
60002	4499	2510	60015
60003	4494	2511	60016
60004	4462	2512	60017
60005	4901		
60006	4466		
60007	4498	2859	61659
60008	4496	2870	61670
60009	4488		
60010	4489	4462	60004
60011	4490	4463	60018
60012	4491	4464	60019
60013	4492	4465	60020
60014	2509	4466	60006
60015	2510	4467	60021
60016	2511	4468	60022
60017	2512	4469	–
60018	4463	4482	60023
60019	4464	4483	60024
60020	4465	4484	60025
60021	4467	4485	60026
60022	4468	4486	60027
60023	4482	4487	60028
60024	4483	4488	60009
60025	4484	4489	60010
60026	4485	4490	60011
60027	4486	4491	60012
60028	4487	4492	60013
60029	4493	4493	60029
60030	4495	4494	60003
60031	4497	4495	60030
60032	4900	4496	60008
60033	4902	4497	60031
60034	4903	4498	60007
		4499	60002
60700	10000	4500	60001
		4900	60032
61659	2859	4901	60005
61670	2870	4902	60033
		4903	60034
		10000	60700

To convert numbers of LMS Class 8P Pacifics into BR listings, add 40,000, eg 6220 became 46220.

INDEX